THE Somerset & Dorset Line
From Above
Evercreech Junction to Bournemouth

THE
Somerset
& Dorset Line
From Above
Evercreech Junction to Bournemouth

KEVIN POTTS | Aerial Photography ALLAN BURNEY and MARK WAGNER AVIATION IMAGES
Additional Colour Images MARK B. WARBURTON

Ian Allan
PUBLISHING

First published 2014

ISBN 978 0 7110 3756 4

Published by Ian Allan Publishing Ltd, Hersham, Surrey KT12 4RG.

Printed in Malta

Visit the Ian Allan Publishing website at www.ianallanpublishing.com

Picture Credits
The present day aerial photographs in this book were taken by Allan Burney and Mark Wagner
and are the copyright of Aviation Images. The historical colour photographs were taken by Mark
B. Warburton and are the copyright of his estate. The Aerofilms pictures are © English Heritage
(Aerofilms Collection).

FRONT COVER Having left Stalbridge the line is now tracking southeast
towards Sturminster Newton. The River Lydden was crossed using Bridge
167, the remains of which can be seen here.

BACK COVER Looking southwest, just north of Cole, nothing now remains
of Bridge 118 where the GWR main line was crossed

PAGE 1 A close up view of Polsham halt, sited just to the left of the road
junction, reveals that the original buildings remain in use as a private
residence. The station was only provided with a single platform and siding.

PAGE 2 An overhead view of Stourpaine positions the site of the halt centrally
in the shot. The A350 angles in from the left, meeting the A357 just by the
stone bridge across the River Stour.

PAGE 3 Bridge 115 at Wyke Champflower was unique to the S&D in that it was
originally constructed to span double track – other bridges were single span
and had a second span added when the line was later doubled.

RIGHT Bournemouth West station; southern terminus of the S&D and journey's
end. Taking advantage of this view from height, the line can be seen passing
the former carriage sidings which now house Bournemouth Traincare Depot.

Contents

Introduction

This is the second 'From Above' volume by Ian Allan Publishing on the Somerset & Dorset Railway. The first volume covered the route of the railway from Bath to Evercreech Junction; this one continues the journey from Evercreech to Bournemouth as well as the branches to Glastonbury, Wells, Bridgwater and Burnham-on-Sea. We hope the readers will enjoy the novel overhead perspective on the route of the railway. Although much of the railway has dissolved into the landscape since the line was closed in 1966, traces remain, sometimes more visible from the air than on the ground. The relationship between the landscape and topography and the railway also becomes apparent from the air. The railway was built with commercial ambitions, but one can see how rural the area is, how the towns and villages are connected in the countryside, and also how many industries made their home in the landscape of Dorset and Somerset. The destination for many travellers, and where this book concludes, is Bournemouth. The seaside drew many holidaymakers coming down from the North and the Midlands on trains such as the 'Pines Express' and Bournemouth's rapid growth in the nineteenth century is largely as a result of the railways as it was also connected directly to London by the London & South Western Railway. Today it rivals many cities in the country.

The railway builders also felt that the north Somerset coast and intervening towns were destinations to aim for, again with an eye to their commercial potential for the Bristol Channel ports, farming, tourism and industry, including the occasional household name such as the shoe manufacturers Clark's, as well as local passengers. Here the landscape is different again – water-filled levels, the mysterious Glastonbury Tor on the horizon, the north Somerset coast. Although in the end the S&D was seen as no longer commercial – or rather, its unprofitability could no longer be supported – and the line was closed, it will be remembered for the huge variety of landscape in its 115 miles, its maintenance of its own character against larger corporate Grouping and Nationalisation interests. As you follow the line through Somerset and Dorset in this book its special nature will be revealed, still evident in the traces in the landscape.

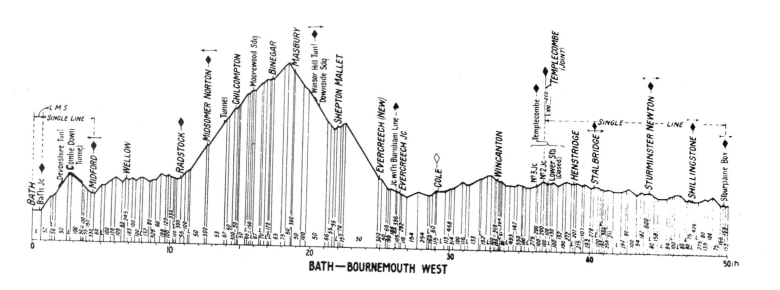

BATH—BOURNEMOUTH WEST

ABOVE A view of Wincanton from the south emphasises the total removal of any railway infrastructure from the modern landscape. The A303 dual carriageway crosses the photograph and seems suspiciously devoid of the usual traffic levels. The railway continues southwards towards Templecombe and its link with the former London & South Western Railway main line.

BELOW Map and gradient profile reproduced from *An Historical Survey of the Somerset & Dorset Railway* by C. W. Judge and C. R. Potts, Oxford Publishing Company, 1979/1988.

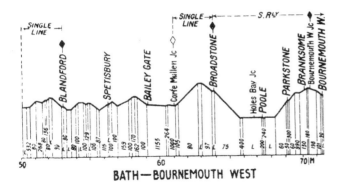

BATH—BOURNEMOUTH WEST

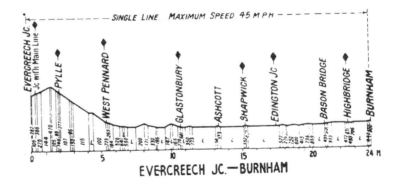

EVERCREECH JC.—BURNHAM

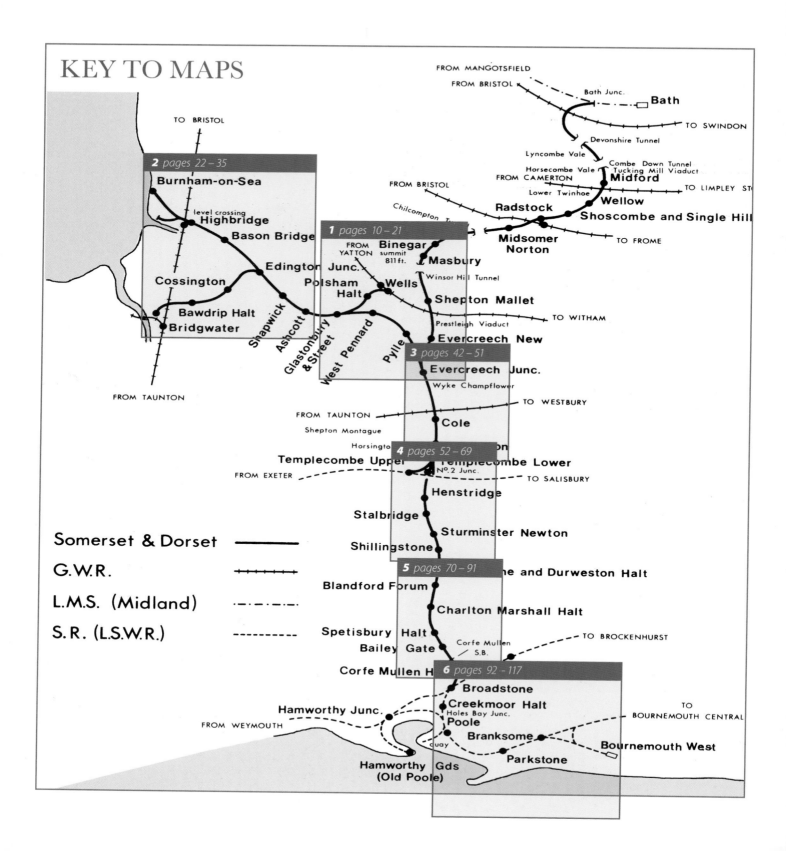

KEY TO MAPS

FROM MANGOTSFIELD

FROM BRISTOL

Bath Junc.

Bath

TO SWINDON

Devonshire Tunnel

Lyncombe Vale

Combe Down Tunnel

Horsecombe Vale

Tucking Mill Viaduct

FROM CAMERTON

Midford

TO LIMPLEY ST

Lower Twinhoe

Wellow

Radstock

Shoscombe and Single Hill

TO BRISTOL

Chilcompton T...

Midsomer Norton

TO FROME

TO BRISTOL

2 *pages 22 – 35*

Burnham-on-Sea

level crossing

Highbridge

Bason Bridge

1 *pages 10 – 21*

FROM YATTON

Binegar summit 811 ft.

Masbury

Winsor Hill Tunnel

Edington Junc.

Cossington

Polsham Halt

Wells

Shepton Mallet

TO WITHAM

Bawdrip Halt

Shapwick

Ashcott

Glastonbury & Street

West Pennard

Pylle

Prestleigh Viaduct

Evercreech New

Bridgwater

3 *pages 42 – 51*

Evercreech Junc.

Wyke Champflower

TO WESTBURY

FROM TAUNTON

FROM TAUNTON

Cole

Shepton Montague

Horsingto...

4 *pages 52 – 69*

Templecombe Upper

Templecombe Lower

No. 2 Junc.

FROM EXETER

TO SALISBURY

Henstridge

Stalbridge

Sturminster Newton

Shillingstone

5 *pages 70 – 91*

...e and Durweston Halt

Blandford Forum

Charlton Marshall Halt

Somerset & Dorset

G.W.R.

L.M.S. (Midland)

S.R. (L.S.W.R.)

Spetisbury Halt

Bailey Gate

Corfe Mullen S.B.

TO BROCKENHURST

Corfe Mullen H...

6 *pages 92 – 117*

Broadstone

Hamworthy Junc.

Creekmoor Halt

Holes Bay Junc.

TO BOURNEMOUTH CENTRAL

FROM WEYMOUTH

Poole

Branksome

TO

quay

Bournemouth West

Hamworthy Gds (Old Poole)

Parkstone

Evercreech Junction to Burnham-on-Sea

Northwest from Evercreech

Before continuing the journey south from Evercreech Junction, a change in both pace and direction will allow closer inspection of the single line running for 24 miles to Burnham-on-Sea and Highbridge. This was originally the S&D's main line until superseded by the Bath extension in 1874, at which point it became 'the Branch'. In contrast to the gradients and curves encountered south of Bath in the first book on the S&D (*The Somerset & Dorset From Above: Bath to Evercreech Junction*, Ian Allan Publishing, 2013), the Branch ran dead straight and virtually level for mile after mile. Looking from the northwest, the main line can be seen approaching the site of Evercreech Junction across the top of the picture before negotiating Pecking Mill curve. Being the original line, the Branch enjoys a straighter alignment as it leaves Evercreech. Curving gently west its path is still marked across today's fields and is easily distinguished from the air. Elbow Corner Crossing is visible with the former crossing keeper's cottage still standing in the bottom of this shot – the reason behind its name is obvious from this height!

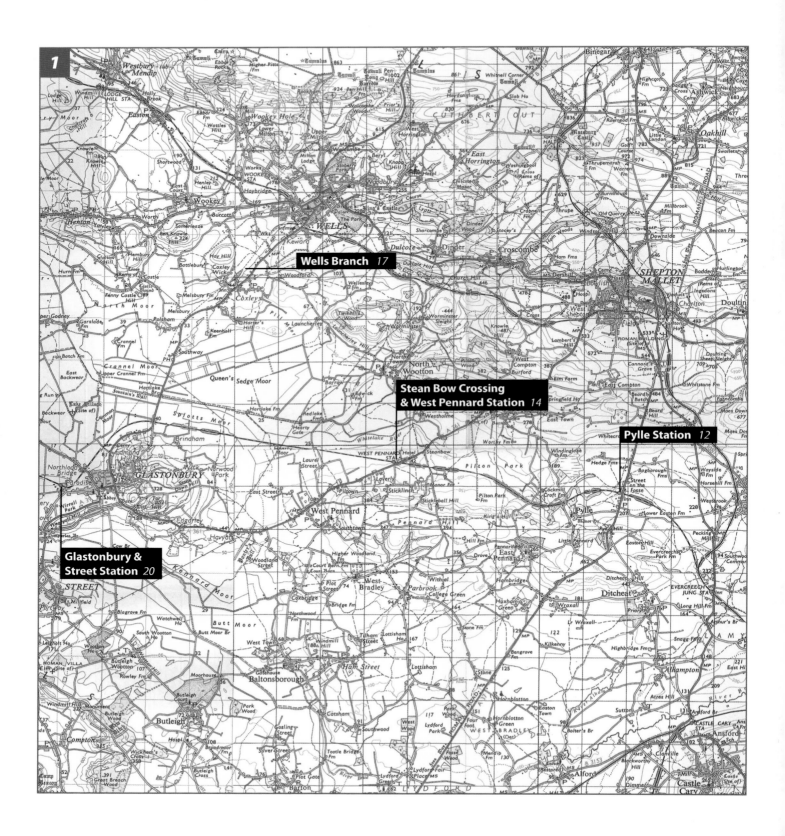

Wells Branch *17*

Stean Bow Crossing & West Pennard Station *14*

Pylle Station *12*

Glastonbury & Street Station *20*

Wells, 1933. The S&D's Well's (Priory Road) station is behind the Diploma Cheese Factory and Wells Public Assistance Institution. The goods shed is also visible to the left of the station. The GWR line branches off top left. *English Heritage (Aerofilms Collection)*

Pylle Station

After leaving Evercreech Junction the line ran for 1¾ miles to the west before arriving at Pylle. Opened in 1862, the station was over a mile from the village it served. Indeed, the line passed closer to the village after it left the station and began descending at a ruling gradient of 1 in 88 towards the Somerset Levels! This was the only notable incline on the Branch.

Pylle station site is hidden from traffic on the A37 by trees. The road crossed the line using Bridge 243, since demolished. Originally constructed with a passing loop, this was removed in 1929 and the station became unstaffed from 1957. Pylle was unusual in that the goods shed – seen here as the larger building in the picture – was also combined with the Station Master's house. This was constructed on the eastern end (right-hand side as seen here) and the whole building has since been converted to residential accommodation. The original station buildings also survive – they too have now been adapted for domestic use – and sit closer to the camera.

West from Pylle

The Royal Bath and West of England Showground can be seen at the top of the picture with Pylle station site just identifiable below it by using the former goods shed as a feature that stands out from the air. From here, the line descends in sweeping curves through Pylle Wood, its path traced by the treeline.

Still looking west, the camera has now moved just beyond the limits of the previous picture and shows the line approaching Stean Bow Crossing with the A361 and West Pennard station just beyond. From there, the Branch can be seen running straight as a die for some 4 miles towards Glastonbury. From this perspective the nature of the Branch clearly contrasts with the line north of Evercreech towards Bath.

Stean Bow Crossing and West Pennard Station

At the end of the gradient from Pylle the line reached West Pennard station. Before doing so it passed over Stean Bow Crossing. In this instance the roadway is more visible from the aerial perspective although the former trackbed can be seen crossing next to the red brick house now occupying the site of the former crossing keeper's cottage. The A361 crosses the centre of the picture running from Shepton Mallet towards Glastonbury. West Pennard station is on the left-hand side of the shot, but hidden from road traffic. A good lead-in feature for those travelling on the A361 is the former Railway Inn – now renamed The Apple Tree – sited on the roadside in the centre of the picture.

As was the case at Pylle, villagers from West Pennard wishing to use the railway faced a long walk to the station: in this instance, almost 2 miles. The station still exists, although it has been taken into private ownership and further developed over the years. Removal of Bridge 257 and realignment of the A361 means that it is no longer visible from the road. After closure of the loop at Pylle in 1929 West Pennard became the Branch's first crossing point

until its own loop was removed in 1964. The up platform had a stone-built booking office and waiting room which can be seen here from the air. So, too can the large stone goods shed, although site development has added to the non-railway infrastructure. The former Station Master's house sits alongside the access road, also now privately occupied. From West Pennard the Branch now ran in a straight line towards Glastonbury.

Wells Branch

The Somerset Central Railway opened the line from Highbridge to Glastonbury in 1854. In 1859 the railway was further extended to the cathedral city of Wells. This the viewpoint allows virtually the whole 5½-mile length of the Wells branch to be seen. It diverges from today's road but then runs roughly parallel to it, heading towards Wells in the upper right area of the shot. The Branch, running in from West Pennard, skirted around the town's northern limits. Its path is now marked by the A39, curving around today's urban development.

ABOVE The only intermediate station on the Wells branch was Polsham, sited 2½ miles before Wells (Priory Road). It sits alongside the A39 road towards the bottom of this picture. The track formation is more difficult to trace as the line gets closer to Wells – hardly surprising since the branch closed to passenger traffic in 1951. Wells Cathedral stands out in the centre of the city.

Unfortunately, the railway only reached the extremities of Wells, a factor which possibly contributed to its demise. And, for those who have arrived here after travelling via the first volume on the S&D from above, that *is* Wells mast on the skyline in the left corner of the shot!

ABOVE At one time Wells' complicated railway history resulted in the city boasting no fewer than three railway stations. The S&D was represented by Wells (Priory Road) with the GWR sited nearby – although for 56 years GWR trains exercised running powers to pass through the S&D station without stopping! Today there is no trace of this infrastructure and Wells has no rail link. The S&D branch ran in, passing to the right of the square green sports field, and terminated in the area now occupied by the industrial units and blue iso-containers. The roundabout that the HGV has just crossed was built on the site of the Station Master's house. The brown industrial unit opposite the iso-containers marks the site of the goods shed which has now been relocated for use on the East Somerset Railway.

To Wells

Glastonbury & Street Station

This panoramic view of Glastonbury illustrates the way in which the S&D skirted around the town's northern extremities, running where the A39 does today, before curving sharply to approach Glastonbury & Street station. The station boasted three platforms, ornate awnings and a covered footbridge. From overhead, the camera shows that all this has now gone. although the entrance to the site is still made through a pair of replica crossing gates. In addition, the Somerset Central Railway used the Abbey Arms and Railway Hotel as company offices until 1877. This building still stands. As a final reminder of the town's railway history, the island platform's wooden canopy has been dismantled and re-erected in the town centre on the site of the open air market.

A closer view of the station site shows – at first glance – no remaining link to one of the S&D's most attractive and spacious stations. Initially opened as Glastonbury, the suffix '& Street' was added in 1886 in recognition of the growing importance of that town, sitting some 2 miles south. The blue containers on the left side of the industrial site mark the position of the station itself, although the area also contained a generous goods yard. Close inspection will reveal that a former engineer's building – just alongside the iso-containers – still remains as a private residence. Trains departing towards the north were faced with an extremely tight curve and subject to a 5mph speed restriction. Although the track formation appeared to be doubled, both the Wells branch and the Evercreech line left as single track and ran side by side until parting at the northern end of town. As can be seen, the line only reached the town's outskirts and never provided convenient access to the centre.

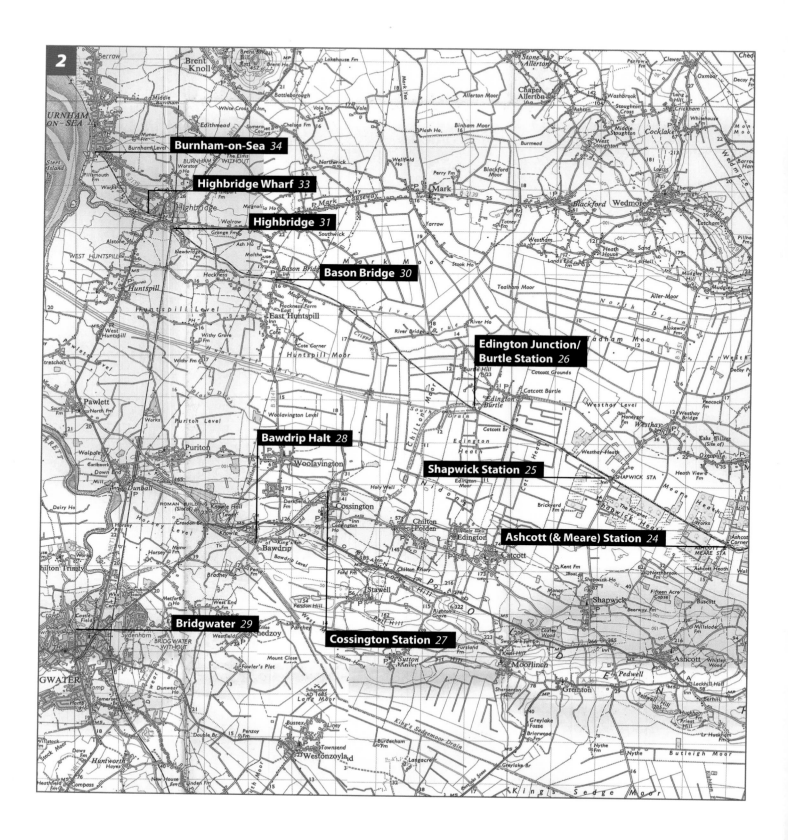

2

Burnham-on-Sea *34*

Highbridge Wharf *33*

Highbridge *31*

Bason Bridge *30*

Edington Junction/ Burtle Station *26*

Bawdrip Halt *28*

Shapwick Station *25*

Ashcott (& Meare) Station *24*

Bridgwater *29*

Cossington Station *27*

Highbridge, 1930. Highbridge Works is at the bottom right, followed by the S&D's station. The S&D then crosses the GWR before heading to Burnham.

Ashcott (& Meare) Station

The panoramic picture of Ashcott Corner illustrates the flat meadows and watercourses, often waterlogged in winter, through which the Branch passed. Ashcott station is visible in the centre of the shot. Sitting on the east side of a lane linking Ashcott (2 miles south) and Meare (1mile north), the station bore both names until 1876. Its early timber platform was replaced by SR concrete and it boasted a single siding for goods traffic. The current bungalow situated on the site was built to replace the former station house. A 2ft narrow gauge line crossed the S&D Branch at right angles ½ mile west of the station site. In 1949 this was the scene of an accident when a local train hit the privately owned petrol-driven narrow gauge engine that had stalled across the Branch in fog. Due to poor access for breakdown cranes the locomotive was cut up on site for removal. Although the station no longer exists, the Railway Inn set along the lane to the top of the shot does and boasts a fine painted locomotive pub sign. No doubt it provided handy sustenance for the breakdown gang!

Shapwick Station

Two miles west of Ashcott the site of Shapwick station retains no clue as to its previous use other than the inevitable name of 'Station Road'. Set in the heart of the Somerset Levels two miles from its village, Shapwick was another crossing point on the Branch. It had two platforms set to the left of the gated road crossing and a small goods yard on the eastern side. This was built to handle peat traffic which was inevitably lost to road transport in later years. Nothing has survived – not even the Griffin's Head Inn marked on earlier OS maps of the line and which sat on the level site at the very bottom of this shot.

Edington Junction/Burtle Station

Almost 17½ miles from Evercreech Junction, this station was opened as Edington Road in 1856 with only a single platform. It was renamed Edington Junction in 1890 when the 7¼-mile single line to Bridgwater opened. The station expanded with the number of platforms being doubled. After the Bridgwater branch closed to passengers (1952) and goods (1954) the station was again renamed as Edington Burtle. The station site is seen towards the bottom of this picture and the junction can still be traced as the Bridgwater line curves away to the left leaving the original line heading off into the

distance towards Highbridge and Burnham-on-Sea. The Station Master's house is now a private dwelling and sits to the right of the former level crossing. The link between rail and ale continues; the Railway Hotel remains as a public house. Situated on the road just to the right of the station site, it has been renamed The Tom Mogg in honour of one of the line's signalmen – the pub sign shows him ringing the hand bell used at the crossing to warn of approaching trains! The former Glastonbury Canal (also now known as the South Drain) stands out clearly as it heads towards the coast.

Cossington Station

This was originally constructed as the only intermediate station on the Bridgwater branch and was well placed for access from the village it served. The line can be seen snaking across the landscape from Edington Junction to pass down the northwestern side of the village. The station is sited in the far apex of the built-up area against the treeline. The substantial grey stone Station Master's house still dominates the country station site. Newer properties have been built in the former goods yard and some of the deep cuttings on the station approaches filled in. The station enjoyed considerable cattle traffic with livestock transported to market at Highbridge and Bridgwater. Although not readily apparent from this angle, the station is close to the summit of a 1 in 72 climb from both directions.

Bawdrip Halt

Villagers in Bawdrip had to wait until 1923 for their halt to be built on the line. Today's aerial scene shows that Bridge 306, carrying the line over Bawdrip Lane, still stands. The station only had a single platform furnished with a small shelter and booking office. This occupied the site on the far right of the shot and backed onto the village hall which could be mistaken for the station buildings. The trackbed from this point up to Bridge 306 forms a garden for the bungalow seen just to the right of the bridge. As a subtle nod to the past, this dwelling has been named 'Essandee'!

Bridgwater

The Bridgwater branch was, in fact, built by the Bridgwater Railway and leased to the S&D. The town generated trade in bricks, tile and cattle as well as passenger traffic and was served by both the S&D and GWR. Looking north, this panoramic view shows the S&D trackbed crossing the M5 motorway at the top right of the picture. It then runs parallel to the A39 Bath Road before crossing the former GWR main line (note Bridgwater station towards the bottom right of shot) and the A38 Bristol Road. No trace of the S&D now remains in the town although its former path can still be traced with the railway's land in Bridgwater now occupied by industrial and retail units. Sainsbury's – seen here to the lower right of the central green area – sits on the station site. The station approaches can be faintly seen crossing the A38 at the top of the picture before running parallel beneath what is now Boards Road. The station area included a large goods yard and single-road engine shed (although in later years motive power was provided from Templecombe). From the goods yard sidings a ½-mile branch curved sharply to the north, turning through 180° to reach wharves on the River Parett. These were situated just below the river bridge in the top left of shot. They fell into disuse after World War 1 and the rails were lifted in World War 2. Bridgwater was renamed Bridgwater North in 1949. The route taken by the GWR line to the docks can be made out as it curves away from the current station.

Bason Bridge

Opened in 1856, Bason Bridge consisted of a single platform and wooden buildings built on the northern side of the River Brue. The station site is in the upper left corner of this picture, beyond the river bridge and road crossing. In 1909 Wilts United Dairies opened a milk factory just to the east of this road which generated substantial traffic for the line and resulted in extra sidings being laid to accommodate this. The dairy site is now occupied by a variety of companies. The former Station Master's house is now a private residence and can be seen at the far left extremity of the station site.

Highbridge

Highbridge was opened in 1854 as part of the Highbridge to Glastonbury section of the Somerset Central Railway, being worked by the Bristol & Exeter Railway until absorption into the S&D in 1862. Trains arriving from Evercreech and Glastonbury ran into the town past Highbridge Works, since demolished and now the site of the huge industrial and storage complex seen just to the west of the M5 motorway. The works eventually became responsible for the repair and maintenance of locomotives and rolling stock for the entire S&D. Following cutbacks and recession the closure of this facility in 1930 made over 300 men redundant – a devastating blow for the town. The GWR main line between Bristol and Taunton can just be seen on the left of the picture.

The station was constructed adjacent to the GWR main line station and sat alongside the River Brue. Trains carrying on towards Highbridge Wharf and Burnham therefore had to traverse GWR metals using a flat crossing which sat beneath Bridge 281 carrying the B3919 over the railway. This bridge can be seen in the centre of the shot. Today there is no trace of the S&D's infrastructure which ultimately totalled five platforms and a three-road carriage shed. Whereas the GWR station remains in much simplified form, the S&D station now lies beneath the housing estate seen to the right of the main line.

Highbridge Wharf

Highbridge Wharf lay ½ mile west of Highbridge station with rail access gained by crossing the busy A38 road. The station site can be identified using the red-brick housing estate to the top right of this shot as a reference point. From here the line to Burnham ran alongside Newtown Road before continuing out to the left of this view following the green belt between the lake and industrial storage yard. The wharf's associated sidings and goods yard sat to the south of this line. Coal, timber, rails and local dairy/agricultural products were handled here in considerable quantities with the S&D even owning its own ships until 1933. Access to the Glastonbury Canal was through the gate of the sea lock. The wharf sidings were closed in 1965 and much of the associated basin infilled. This now forms the newer red-brick housing estate seen in the centre of the picture and running parallel to the canal.

Burnham-on-Sea

LEFT Journey's end on the Branch is reached 24 miles from Evercreech Junction. The camera sits high offshore looking east over Burnham-on-Sea. Having now (hopefully) developed a practised eye, the former S&D line can be traced back from the pier, through the town centre and out towards Highbridge. The formation now forms part of a road for much of the way. The site of the former Highbridge Works stands out in the distance to help.

ABOVE As the terminus of a Georgian resort, Burnham station, opened in 1858, was graced with an overall roof. The station buildings sat on the site now decorated by ornamental stones seen adjacent to the road junction in the centre of this shot. The original platform was only 88 yards in length and so an excursion platform of 225 yards was added to cope with this traffic. The station was renamed Burnham-on-Sea in 1923 to attract holidaymakers to the resort. Although the line ran out onto the pier, this was sold in 1905. Regular passenger traffic ceased in 1951 although excursions continued to use the branch until 1962. After closure the station's small signalbox was relocated to Washford station on the West Somerset Railway by the S&D Railway Trust. Although no railway infrastructure remains today, the S&D is not forgotten; the 'Somerset & Dorset Inn' still displays appropriate signage. It can be found at the corner of the road junction opposite the station site. Ideal, perhaps, for a drink and the opportunity to reflect on the unique nature of the Branch before heading back to Evercreech Junction for the journey south towards Bournemouth?

PYLLE
GWR 0-6-0 No 2210 accelerates away from Pylle station towards Evercreech Junction on 28 April 1962 with a Great Western style B set illustrating the effect of the transfer of responsibility for the Somerset & Dorset to the Western Region. *Mark Warburton*

PYLLE
At Pylle station, the Glastonbury to Templecombe extension of the Somerset Central passed under the A37, which here was on the alignment of the Roman Fosse Way. Taken on the same day as the previous photograph, this unusual angle of No 2210 and its train stopped in the station shows the simple station building on the right, the combined station masters house and goods shed and the rear of the signalbox.
Mark Warburton

WEST PENNARD
Ivatt 2-6-2T No 41242 starts a
substantial train from Highbridge
of five carriages away from West
Pennard station on 21 July 1962
with a good head of steam to
tackle the four miles at 1 in 86
to reach Pylle. From left to right
can be seen the station master's
house; the main station building,
the signalbox and the wooden
shelter on the platform; and
the substantial goods shed.
Mark Warburton

WEST PENNARD
The fireman on Collett 0-6-0
No 2219 awaits the single-line
tablet for the section to
Glastonbury alongside the
signalbox at West Pennard on
21 July 1962. Similarly shaped
barge boards were also seen on
signalboxes at Highbridge and
Burnham and at Glastonbury
station. The flower bed in the
foreground shows plenty of
evidence of the business of station
duties here! *Mark Warburton*

GLASTONBURY
Midland Railway 3F 0-6-0 No 43427 was built by Dubs in 1892 and still had two more years of service when photographed at Glastonbury on a Highbridge to Evercreech Junction service on 15 August 1959. Plenty of evidence of goods traffic is visible on the right and in the sidings visible in the distance under the footbridge.
Mark Warburton

GLASTONBURY
The winter sun shines on Ivatt 2-6-2T No 41307 on pilot duty resting behind the signalbox at Glastonbury on 16 December 1965. The shunter has leant his pole against the engine while he talks to the footplate staff, or perhaps negotiates a chance to warm up. *Mark Warburton*

GLASTONBURY

Ivatt 2-6-2T is about to leave Glastonbury for Highbridge on 16 December 1965. The signalman makes his way back to the signalbox, while the driver examines the single-line tablet he has handed over and the guard closes his van doors. The drinking water containers were necessary as a number of the crossing houses had no mains water so relied on fresh water being carried to them on service trains. *Mark Warburton*

SHAPWICK

The porter has walked down the platform to Ivatt 2-6-2T No 41296 to exchange the single-line tablets as a Highbridge to Templecombe train stops at Shapwick on 1 June 1963. Lower quadrant LSWR signal arms are much in evidence, as is the South Drain to the right. *Mark Warburton*

HIGHBRIDGE

GWR 0-6-0 No 2204 rolls into the arrival platform at Highbridge on Saturday 22 June 1963 with a train from Evercreech Junction, passing Ivatt 2-6-2T No 41296 in the departure platform. Somebody has been doing some cleaning to reveal the copper cap of the chimney of the Collett 0-6-0.
Mark Warburton

HIGHBRIDGE CROSSING

GWR 0-6-0 No 2204 returns from Burnham empty stock over the level crossing at Highbridge East B signalbox on Saturday 21 July 1962. The connecting points to the GWR line can be seen just in front of the tender; however, this train is returning to Highbridge Somerset & Dorset to work a return train to Evercreech Junction (and presumably to drop off the passengers on the footplate). In the background is the GWR goods depot and on the right the private siding into A. G. Pitts brick and tile works of this area. *Mark Warburton*

BURNHAM

In the school holidays, one service train a day was extended from Highbridge to Burnham-on-Sea from the closure to regular passengers in October 1951 until September 1962. GWR 0-6-0 No 2204 arrives at Burnham on Saturday 21 July 1962 past a variety of local coal merchant's lorries indicating a healthy domestic coal market which kept the goods service going to May 1963. *Mark Warburton*

BURNHAM

GWR 0-6-0 No 2204 emerges from the covered station at Burnham-on-Sea on Saturday 21 July 1962 with the competition evident on the left in the form of a brace of Midland Red coaches. Judging by the coats and sweaters, summers 50 years ago were no better than today! *Mark Warburton*

Evercreech Junction to Bournemouth

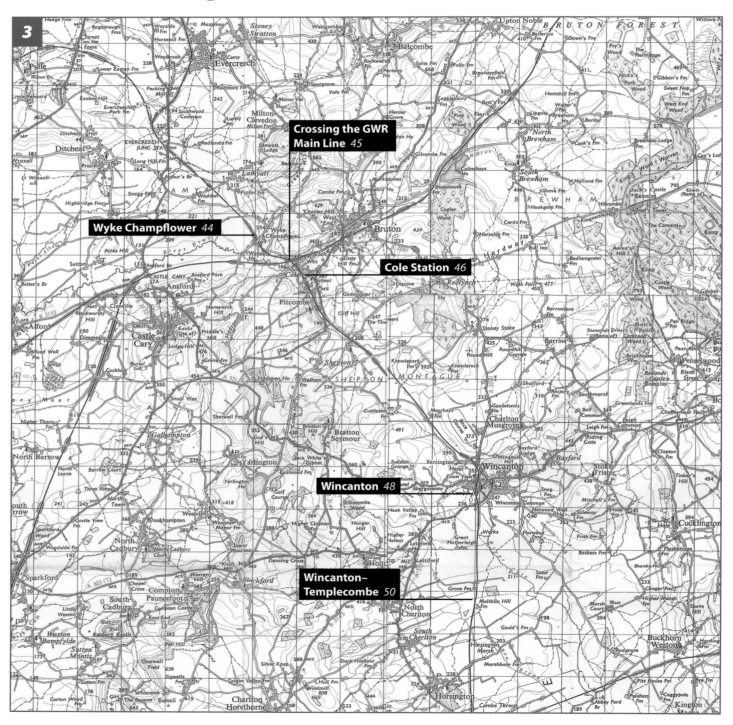

Crossing the GWR
Main Line *45*

Wyke Champflower *44*

Cole Station *46*

Wincanton *48*

Wincanton–
Templecombe *50*

Wincanton, 1937. The S&D station, sidings and the Cow and Gate Factory are clearly visible. *English Heritage (Aerofilms Collection)*

Wyke Champflower

Leaving Evercreech Junction and heading south the Mendip Hills recede into the distance and the countryside begins to flatten out. With the Mendips forming the backdrop in this picture, the site of the West of England Showground south of Shepton Mallet can be made out in the middle distance. Evercreech is visible as the large town to the right and Evercreech Junction nearer the camera towards the left of the view. From here the line can be traced running south to pass just to the west of the village of Wyke

Champflower, the outskirts of which appear on the right hand side of the shot. Bridge 115 carried Wyke Road over the line and this is visible towards the bottom centre of the picture at the point where the road, running left to right, crosses the treeline. This was unique to the S&D in that it was originally constructed to span double track – other bridges were single span and had a second span added when the line was later doubled. The bridge remains in situ but has been partially infilled, as can be seen in this view.

Crossing the GWR Main Line

The S&D line crossed Great Western Railway metals for the fifth – and final – time since leaving Bath just to the north of Cole. This location has historic significance to the line; it is the point at which the Somerset Central Railway met with the Dorset Central Railway in 1862 to create a link between the Bristol Channel (via the then Highbridge 'main line') and the South Coast. The two companies merged to form the Somerset & Dorset Railway later that year. The original plan had been to link with the Wiltshire, Somerset & Weymouth Railway (taken over by the GWR in 1850) at a point just beyond the left of this overhead shot. This was abandoned in favour of the link to the Dorset Central, leaving the line south with a sharp curve to the east before reversing right to cross over the GWR main line by means of Bridge 118. The curve meant a permanent speed restriction of 45mph for engine crews. The point at which the GWR line was crossed is conveniently marked here using a passing HST! Cole is just beyond camera shot to the right, but the remnants of the embankment leading to the former Cole Viaduct can be seen to the right (south) of the GWR main line.

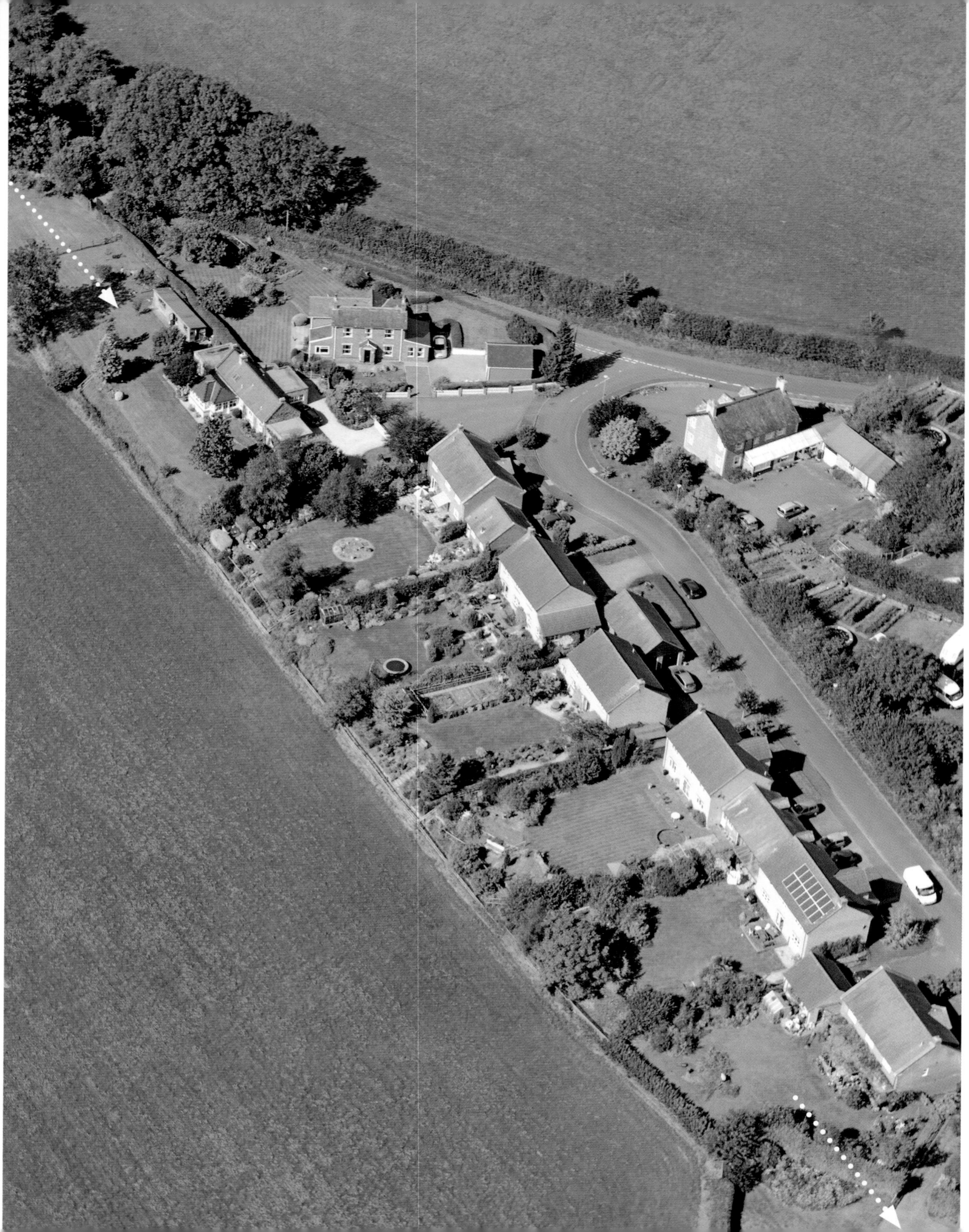

Cole Station

LEFT Cole station is now a private residence but little trace now remains of the station's platforms and the trackbed has been filled in. Lying just over 28½ miles from Bath Road Junction the station buildings on the former down platform at the top of this view and were originally constructed by the Dorset Central Railway, typified by that company's style of high gables and tall chimneys. The Station Master's house faces the camera although the structure has been added to over the years. The large building to the right is the former Railway Hotel, again now in private use. A small housing estate has been built on the site of the former goods yard, the gardens of which extend across the trackbed.

ABOVE The northern section of the S&D – with the dramatic climb to Masbury summit – often featured widely in photographs of the line. Yet the railway was also remarkable for the variation in landscape it experienced over a relatively short distance. The line's southern section passed through unspoilt rural countryside, much of which still retains that charm today. To the south of the station, Mill Lane was carried over the railway on Bridge 121, a two-arch structure situated where the treeline now lies. The cutting has since been filled in but the path taken by the trackbed can be easily traced to Pitcombe Viaduct which can be seen here. Just out of camera shot to the south Bridge 123 still straddles the lane. However, Bridge 124, which crossed the A359 Yeovil-Bruton road, has long since been demolished.

Wincanton

From an operating perspective, running over the southern section of the railway was easier than the north; adverse gradients were comparatively mild and there were even some relatively long straight sections of track by S&D standards! Looking north the village of Shepton Montague sits in the foreground. The line stretches away to pass between the two hills in the middle distance – Cole lies hidden behind the one to the right. As usual, the showground south of Shepton Mallet stands out. The minor road between Shepton Montague and Stoney Stoke runs across the bottom of the picture (just above the tennis court) and crosses the track formation by means of Bridge 127. This bridge, hidden in the treeline, is noteworthy for its clearance of 21ft 2in over the railhead – unlike most other bridges and tunnels on the S&D where headroom was restricted. From Shepton Montague the line ran straight for almost two miles. It was paralleled for some of that distance by a minor road, allowing the more adventurous – and affluent – photographer to experiment with tracking shots of trains taken from a moving car!

Approaching Wincanton the line turned briefly to the east and then due south to pass down the town's western side. No trace of the railway remains today. This wide angled view enables its path to be traced as it cuts diagonally across the shot, crossing the modern day A303 by the blue buildings before continuing to the south, its passage marked by trees. As well as horsebox traffic destined for the nearby racecourse, Wincanton was base to the Cow and Gate Dairy which sent milk by rail to London via the link at Templecombe. The station had staggered platforms, linked by a footbridge, and a small goods yard to the eastern side. Housing now covers the station site although names such as Pines Close offer clues to the historian as to the land's former use. Using the playing field beyond the cemetery as a reference, the line of tall developed green trees marks the beginning of the station area. This extends southwards towards the former dairy buildings. The line crossed the old A303 roadway by means of Bridge 137, now swept away. The line's formation to the south has been submerged beneath industrial development and the modern A303 bypass road. To the south of this feature, farmland has been re-established.

Wincanton – Templecombe

After leaving Wincanton the railway ran due south for three miles, passing through open countryside towards the village of Horsington, just north of Templecombe. Broadmoor Lane crossed the trackbed at Horsington Crossing, seen here at the bottom left of the picture. Once again the former trackbed has been developed to provide a suitable location for rural residential property! Wincanton remains visible as the sprawling built up area in the far distance to the north.

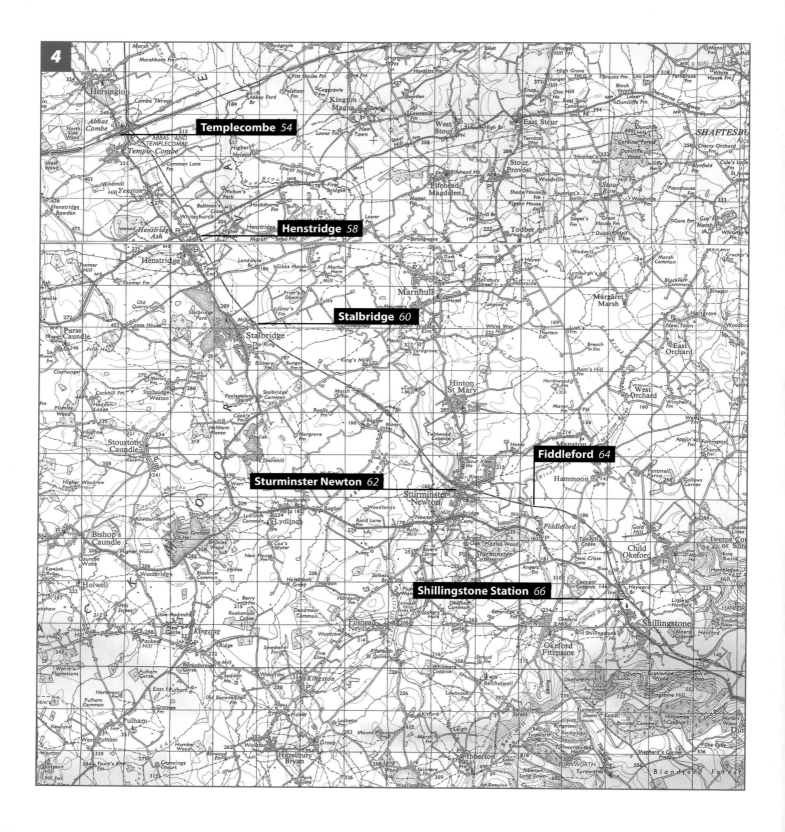

4

Templecombe 54

Henstridge 58

Stalbridge 60

Sturminster Newton 62

Fiddleford 64

Shillingstone Station 66

Templecombe, 1972. Although the S&D had closed by this date, evidence of the railway is still visible at this important interchange. The LSWR main line runs along the top of the photograph and the S&D came in on its embankment from the top left. The BR-built S&D engine shed stands out.
English Heritage (Aerofilms Collection)

Templecombe

Templecombe was once a busy and important railway interchange, despite its rural surroundings. The S&D ran in from the north, intersecting at 90° with the LSWR's main line to the West of England as the latter passed through the village from the east. Although operating procedure and track layout was modified in the early years, the connection remained an awkward and time consuming affair. The S&D dropped sharply to pass beneath a minor road and the LSWR main line. Between the two bridges was a single short platform – Templecombe Lower – which was able to accommodate only two coaches and saw infrequent use. A short spur left the S&D formation just south of Horsington Crossing, running on an embankment that curved sharply to the west before running into Platform 3 on the up side of the LSWR station. With the camera positioned high above Templecombe and facing east, the LSWR line can be seen heading out towards Gillingham and Salisbury. Despite a resurgence in traffic over recent years this line too is a shadow of its former self. Indeed, Templecombe Upper station was closed along with the S&D, leaving only the art deco style signal box in use. This is visible on the opposite side of the track from the present day station car park. Fortunately, local pressure and public demand resulted in the station reopening in 1983, albeit on a smaller scale. Much of the wooded area towards the bottom of the shot was previously occupied by an extensive upper goods yard which saw much interchange traffic from the S&D's lower goods yard. The S&D approached over the ground now occupied by the industrial units seen on the centre left of the shot.

The viewpoint has now been repositioned to the northeast and focuses on what was the S&D's land as it approached Templecombe from the north. Today the site is dominated by Thales Underwater Systems with many new buildings erected on the site of the lower goods yard and engine shed. Incredibly, this latter building still stands although it has been incorporated into the Thales complex. The shed was rebuilt in 1950 as a two-road brick structure. Although provided eventually with a 50ft turntable, this proved too short for larger locomotives. The '7Fs', arriving with goods traffic from Bath, were often forced to return tender first as far as Evercreech Junction, utilising the turntable there before continuing their journey. The S&D was connected to the LSWR line via a short chord leading up to Templecombe Upper station. This now forms part of the access road to the Thales site, it arcs around the school and church seen just to the north of the former LSWR station. It may be cause for some concern that the journey south from Evercreech Junction to Templecombe has, so far, failed to highlight any public houses! To rectify this, readers should identify a building marked by five white windows on its upper level which sits just alongside the point at which the S&D chord joins Templecombe Station. This building faces an ale house that, until recently, was the *Royal Wessex*, complete with pub sign depicting one of Bulleid's magnificent West Country locomotives!

Gartell Light Railway

ABOVE The line's trackbed now passes through open countryside as it heads south towards Henstridge. The line from here was single track for 16 miles until Blandford Forum. Hidden from motorists on the parallel A357 lies the Gartell Light Railway, part of which now runs along the former trackbed. Situated just beyond Yenston, this private railway is owned by the Gartell family whose agricultural and plant machinery business has provided the foundation for this 2ft narrow gauge line. Entrance to the railway is made from Common Lane, passing through the commercial yard associated with the owner's business. The railway's terminus is reached via a fully signalled crossing and covered footbridge from the spacious car park. From here the line rises at 1 in 30 to join the S&D trackbed and runs for over ¾ mile to the south. The climb, and curvature of the line, ensures that the railway's two steam locomotives give a rousing performance as they lift their trains up onto the old S&D formation. Common Lane crossing keeper's house still exists and can be seen in the upper left area of the photograph.

RIGHT A view of the Gartell Light Railway's terminus area clearly shows the amount of railway infrastructure that has been put in place. The line has a large refreshment room, shop and railwayana display. One of the country's leading railwayana auction firms uses the facilities for an annual event which normally includes a strong S&D range of artefacts. The line opens to the public on several running days each year and, as the picture shows, sits in attractive surroundings. Movements are controlled by fully equipped signalboxes and adoption of full sized practice has resulted in some impressive semaphore signal gantries.

BELOW The camera is now repositioned to the north, allowing the trackbed to be traced south beyond Common Lane Crossing. Henstridge can be seen sitting to the right of the line's path in the middle distance and, further still, Stalbridge is just visible.

Henstridge

ABOVE Henstridge station was situated on the eastern side of the village it served and was two miles south of Templecombe. The line's smallest station (and the last before crossing into Dorset), it had only a single platform on the up side and no crossing loop. The goods yard consisted of a single siding, accessed by means of a groundframe. Looking south, the A30 Shaftesbury road cuts across the centre of the picture, intersecting with the A357 that has paralleled the railway out of Templecombe to the right of the view. The A30 crossed the line on Bridge 159. It still stands, but all traces of the station are gone, replaced by the row of brick houses just beyond the A30 and to the right of the trackbed. Looking further south, Stalbridge can be seen in the distance.

RIGHT The view now changes, looking back to the north from just inside the Dorset county border. Henstridge can be clearly seen, the former station site less so. Bridge 161 carrying Landshire Lane over the trackbed remains in place. The rural, relatively undulating nature of the countryside is apparent from this shot.

Stalbridge

ABOVE Stalbridge was the first station inside Dorset for southbound traffic. The station buildings, situated on the up platform, were of brick construction and a long loop was provided for trains to cross on the single-line section. This view looks towards the west and allows the trackbed to be traced from Henstridge (seen in the upper right corner) down the eastern side of Stalbridge through the area now covered by the industrial units.

FACING PAGE TOP Nothing now remains of Stalbridge station; the site is occupied by the factory units seen in the centre of the shot. Station Road was crossed by means of a gated level crossing. Not readily visible in this photograph but stubbornly defying time, a pair of rails lie buried in the roadway just beyond the entry gate to the site. The up platform was unique in that it dipped in the centre, allowing passengers to cross the line by means of a wooden walkway since the station had no footbridge.

FACING PAGE INSET Having left Stalbridge (40 miles from Bath Road Junction) the line is now tracking southeast towards Sturminster Newton. The River Lydden was crossed using Bridge 167, the remains of which can be seen in the photograph. Although easily visible from the air, the nearest road track passes ¼ mile away and so the remaining stone abutments and earthworks lie largely out of sight from the ground.

Sturminster Newton

ABOVE Lying 43¾ miles from Bath and four miles southeast of Stalbridge, the market town of Sturminster Newton sits on high ground surrounded on three sides by the River Avon. Approaching from the right side of the picture, southbound trains made the first of four crossings of the river. Two of the flood arches belonging to Bridge 171 can still be seen in the centre of the shot. The wrought iron lattice centre span has been demolished but, just beyond, the pedestrian footbridge is still in use. This bridge provided a vantage point to capture S&D trains as they departed Sturminster Newton heading north, encapsulated in an idyllic country setting. The single line trackbed leads off to Sturminster Newton beyond the wooded area to the left. It originally ran into a short, steep-sided cutting before reaching the station; this has now been filled in.

RIGHT Sturminster Newton was a busy market town generating cattle and milk traffic for the railway. The line ran into the town through the site now occupied by the builder's yard, under Bridge 172 and the B3092 Bath Road then continuing over the recreation park at the top of the picture. Again, this area has been filled in since the railway's closure. The previously mentioned pedestrian footbridge over the River Stour stands out from this viewpoint. Elements of the town's history have been preserved with a working flour mill creating a link to the past. However, the railway's presence has been eliminated and the former station site is now a car park.

Fiddleford

ABOVE Leaving Sturminster Newton behind, the S&D trackbed heads southeast, maintaining the low ground and following the line of the Stour Valley towards Shillingstone and Blandford Forum. The next crossing of the River Stour is at Fiddleford Mill. Looking from the north, the line of the trackbed is readily visible. A modern footbridge has replaced Bridge 175, allowing use of the formation as a path and cycleway. The original bridge was a five-span wrought iron structure with a lattice main girder section. Fiddleford Mill and weir can be seen towards the top of the picture.

RIGHT Midway between Sturminster Newton and Shillingstone the trackbed sweeps right towards the south. Tan-Hill Copse is the wooded area now beginning to encroach upon the line. The minor road was originally carried over the line by a bridge, now infilled. The cycleway has been maintained by temporarily leaving the formation to cross at the roadway itself. Perhaps the silver car, parked on the former bridge, is another S&D historian exploring the past?

Shillingstone Station

ABOVE Shillingstone village sits at the northern end of the Stour gap through which the river, A357 and railway all pass en route to Blandford Forum. The station lies at the northern extremity of the village it serves, although nearby Child Okeford and Okeford Fitzpaine also provided agricultural and passenger traffic. Taken from the north, the trackbed crosses over the minor road to Child Okeford. Bridge 180 – seen on the right of the picture – is still standing.

FACING PAGE Shillingstone station is now the headquarters of the North Dorset Railway Trust. The organisation is restoring the station and its surroundings with the ultimate aim of continuing to lay track and create a running line through the station site. Lying 46¾ miles from Bath, the station was constructed with red brick buildings on the up platform and finished with an ornate canopy. This was reputed to have been provided for King Edward VII who used the station to visit nearby Iwerne Minster House. Shillingstone was also known for its ornate gardens and these too have been faithfully recreated (along with the station greenhouse), as can be seen from this shot. Access to the site is signposted from the A357, passing along the top of the picture. At the time of the photo, a BR BSK Mk1 carriage sits in the loading dock with a Ruston & Hornsby diesel shunter – resplendent in S&D Prussian blue – under the tarpaulin on the main line. This picture also shows the frames of '9F' 2-10-0 No 92207 under cover in the former goods yard.

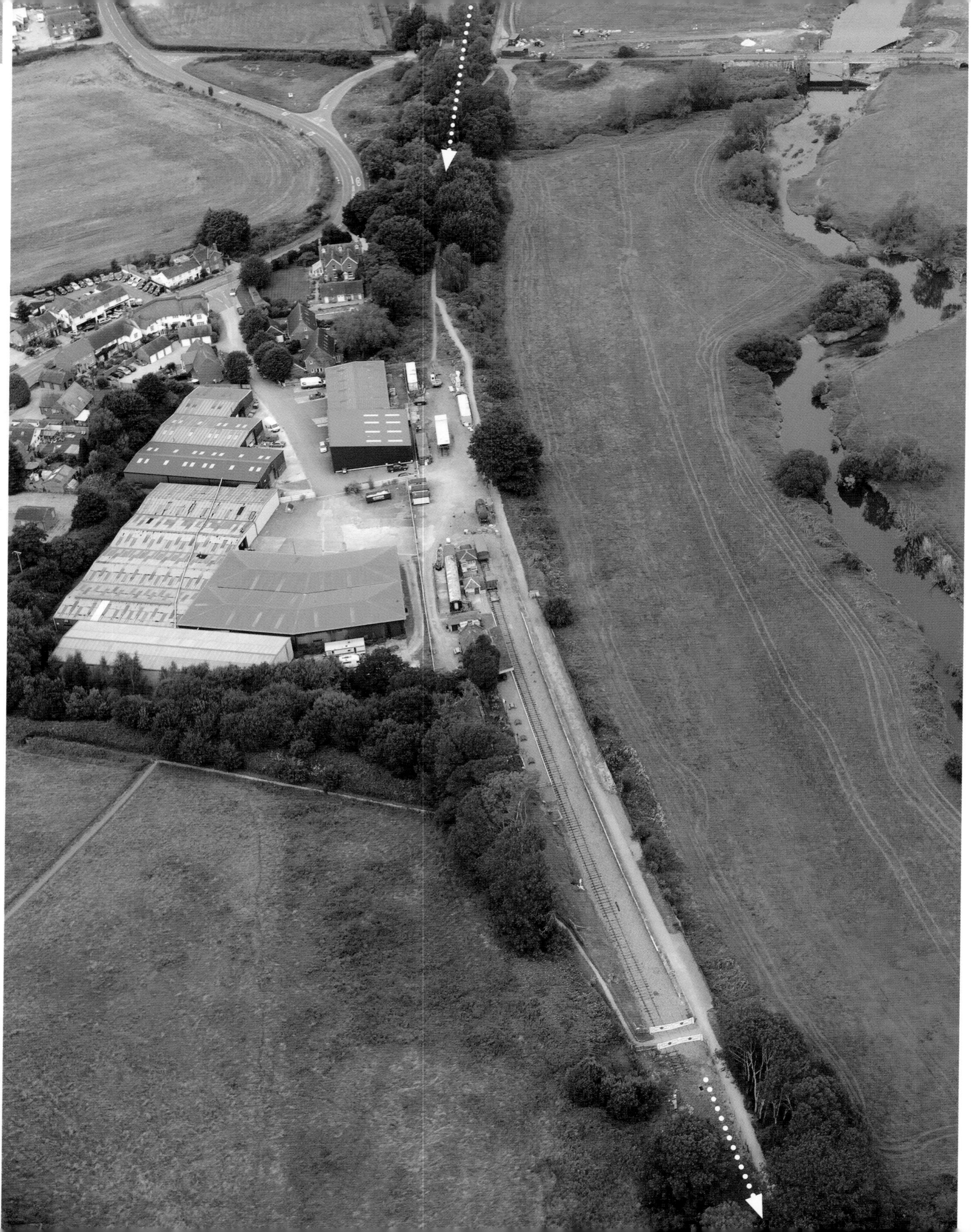

LEFT Shillingstone station now sits on the North Dorset Trailway, a recreational path extending southwards for 7½ miles from Stalbridge along the line of the former trackbed. The pathway can be seen running between the fenced off section of the down platform and the green field. This overhead view of the entire Shillingstone station site highlights the proximity to the River Stour. The southern limit of the North Dorset Railway Trust is marked by the pair of restored crossing gates seen at the bottom of the picture. The pathway provides a delightfully scenic and tranquil route into the Stour Valley, passing a station so iconic that a major model railway manufacturer has recently released it in OO form!

ABOVE Shillingstone itself straddles the A357 for a mile, as can be seen in this shot taken from the southeast. The line can be seen running up the Stour Valley to the station site, just beyond the wooded area.

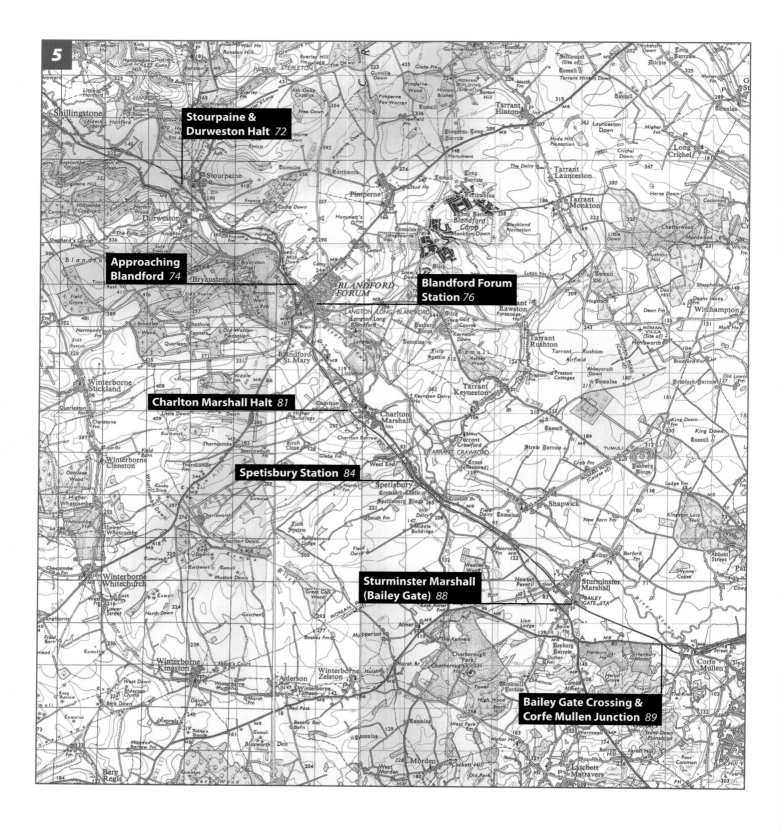

5

Stourpaine & Durweston Halt *72*

Approaching Blandford *74*

Blandford Forum Station *76*

Charlton Marshall Halt *81*

Spetisbury Station *84*

Sturminster Marshall (Bailey Gate) *88*

Bailey Gate Crossing & Corfe Mullen Junction *89*

Blandford Forum, 1930. The S&D line runs above the town in this photograph alongside the River Stour. *English Heritage (Aerofilms Collection)*

Stourpaine & Durweston Halt

LEFT Following the line of the Stour Valley, the trackbed threads its way from Shillingstone – near the top of the picture – to Stourpaine, seen at the bottom. Blandford Forest sits to the left of this view whilst Hod Hill lies just out of shot to the right, providing a funnel feature that guides the line's path. The River Stour is crossed once more by southbound trains at the right-angled intersection of the two treelines just beyond Stourpaine. Looking beyond this point, spoil from the Blandford bypass road has been used to fill in the steep cutting that was previously spanned by the three-arch Cliff Bridge at Gains Cross. This carried a farm track over the line at the furthest apex of the brown triangular field. Stourpaine & Durweston Halt was situated in the site now overgrown with vegetation that can be seen just beyond the green tarpaulin visible

towards the bottom of the picture. The halt was a simple prefabricated concrete structure built in Southern Railway style. At only 120ft in length, the platform had a single shelter on the down side.

ABOVE Looking from the northwest at more detail at features described in the previous caption, the crossing over the River Stour before reaching Stourpaine is shown here. The original railway viaduct has been demolished but a replacement structure has been put in place for users of the North Dorset Trailway. The A357 parallels the railway's path at it heads towards its junction with the A350 and Blandford Forum.

Approaching Blandford

As the railway leaves Stourpaine it follows the contours of the hills encroaching from the east before turning through a long, sweeping curve to the south. The approach to Blandford Forum was through a cutting with the line descending at 1 in 80 over the last ¾ mile before arriving at the station. This was conveniently close to the town centre. Today, as the camera looks back towards the northwest, the line's path is still marked although the Blandford bypass cuts through it as it approaches the town's outskirts.

Blandford Forum Station

The town of Blandford Forum marks the end of the 16-mile single line section from Templecombe. From here the S&D heads south as double track for the next eight miles to Corfe Mullen. With the camera airborne high over Blandford Forum, the line's final destination can just be seen in the top left of the picture as the broad expanse of Poole Bay appears some 15 miles to the south. The town is bounded by the River Stour on its western side and the relatively new Blandford bypass to the southeast. The railway, running parallel to the Stour, can be traced through the town centre by following the treeline until it reaches the square flat-topped building on the far extremity of the built up area.

The camera has now zoomed into the former station site itself, viewed from the southeast. The line's path can be traced using the treeline. As it enters from the right it passes beneath Salisbury Road (Bridge 193) regaining double track at a point abeam the large rectangular building. Bridge 194 can be seen still standing next to the former Station Master's house (faced in white). There is a tentative link to the town's railway past with a single, short length of track and a bufferstop positioned beneath the bridge. The station had its main buildings on the up platform with a goods yard to the eastern side which is now the site of the car park seen in the lower left of the picture. The station area is now occupied by modern housing – again seen in the same area of this shot. Named 'The Sidings', at least some railway link has been maintained. Blandford station (it was renamed Blandford Forum only in 1953) was unusual in that there was no station footbridge. Passengers crossing the line were provided in a subway from the platform. The bridge in this view – from which many photographs were taken – is in fact a public footbridge just to the north of the station site.

As the line approached the town's southern limits the River Stour was crossed for the last time by means of a lattice girder bridge similar to the one at Sturminster Newton. Although this structure (Bridge 198) is now gone, the two northern arches remain and can be seen at the centre of the picture. The approach to this bridge now provides the site for the Co-operative store, seen as the square flat-topped building. The line of trees just before the river mark the site of a short spur which once ran to the nearby army camp. It had a short existence; laid in 1919, it was redundant by 1921 and removed in 1928.

Charlton Marshall Halt

Zooming in towards the station site, the A350 is off to the left of the picture. The former trackbed, now a cycleway and public path, parallels the road. Bridge 203 still carries the connecting road over the trackbed. The station was only provided with rudimentary facilities and steps from the road gave access to the short platforms. The halt still has its platforms – the path leading to the down platform can just be distinguished by the distinctively coloured tree. From the air the overgrowth is such that a shot from almost directly above is necessary to see this.

LEFT From Blandford Forum south to Corfe Mullen the S&D enginemen faced no severe, prolonged gradients and no extreme curves. Consequently this section of the line saw some fast running. The trackbed follows the River Stour and is paralleled by the A350. It is easily traced from Blandford Forum (seen here at the top of the picture) where it passed over the site now occupied by Tesco and other industrial units before running close down the western side of Charlton Marshall. The village only acquired its station in the form of a halt in 1928. It had a relatively short lifespan, closing in 1956, and sat at the far corner of the built up area as seen from this shot. Charlton Marshall stretches out for almost a mile with the railway, cut into the hillside above the village, overlooking the River Stour in the lower ground to the east. The Charlton Inn forms a suitable reference point in this shot. Set almost centrally, the Inn's white building and large car park are easily visible from the air just by the s-bend on the A350. Tracking to the left corner of shot from this point, the station sits in the trees at the apex of the residential area.

RIGHT Continuing south from Charlton Marshall the line sits on a shelf cut into the chalk hillside. It follows the narrow Stour gap which, in turn, means that the village of Spetisbury is linear in nature. In this view the railway can be traced by following the treeline as it runs parallel with the A350, cutting through the lower corner of Spetisbury Rings/Crawford Castle (the Iron Age hill fort). It then crosses the road just before reaching Sturminster Marshall at the top of the picture.

Spetisbury Station

ABOVE Spetisbury station was conveniently sited close to the main road although access to the railway required a steep climb up to the platforms. The station, situated some 1½ miles beyond Charlton Marshall, was closed in 1956. Prior to that, traffic was such that it was reduced to unmanned status and renamed Spetisbury Halt in 1934. This view shows the short access road leading off the A350 with the line carried overhead on Bridge 215. Today the railway is shielded from the view of traffic on the A350 by a combination of its elevated position and extensive vegetation. Circling overhead the station site it is clear that there is now no evidence of the halt itself. However, the access steps leading to the former up platform remain and are situated just behind the left of the bridge

RIGHT Careful observation of this photograph will just reveal the platform access steps leading from the small yellow square and bonnet of the parked car. It is interesting to note that photographs taken from the platform when the line was in use often capture the main road in the background – gloriously uncluttered with road traffic and signage!

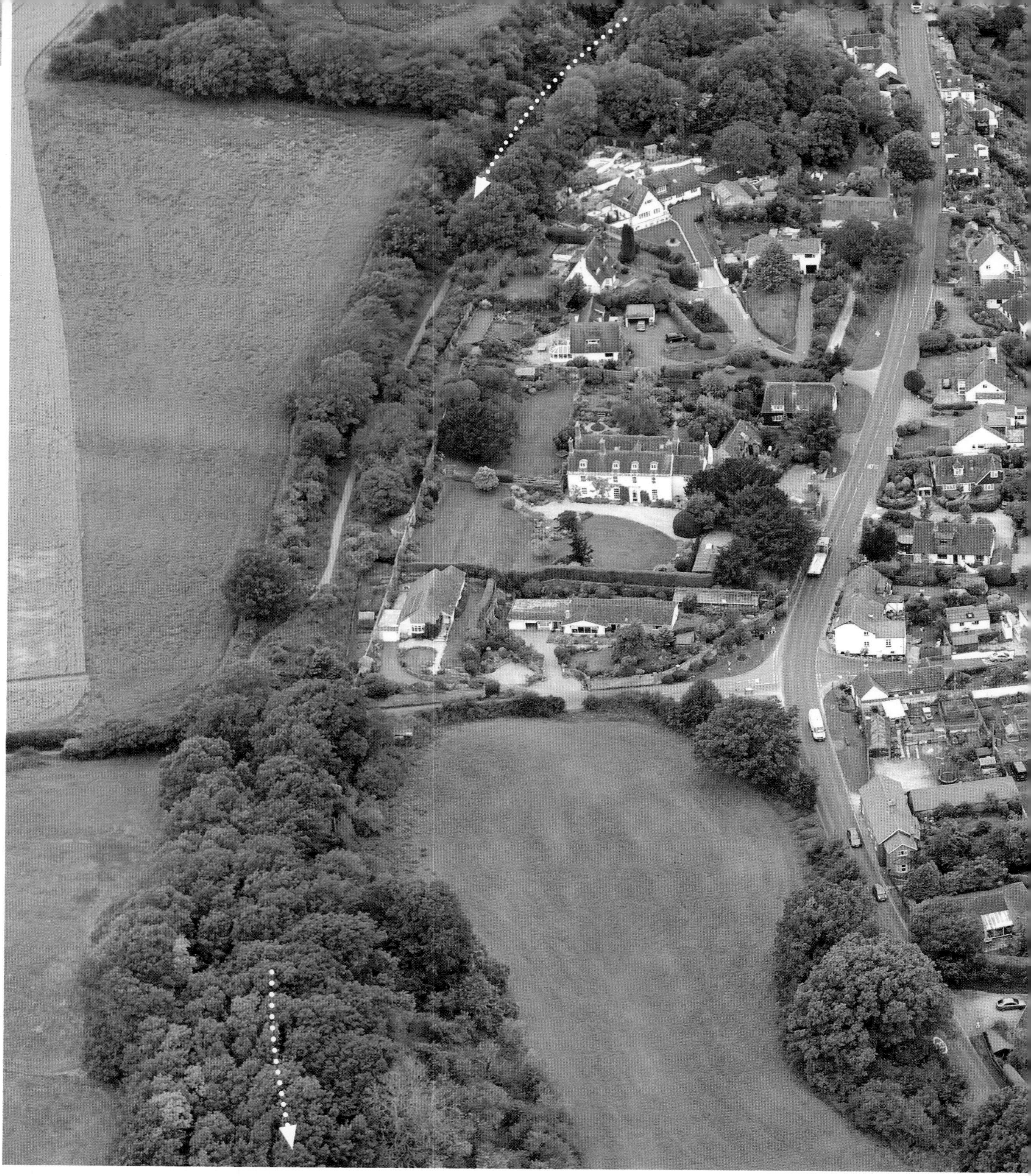

As the train departed Spetisbury those passengers travelling south over the S&D must have felt growing excitement now that the holiday destination of Bournemouth was only 15 miles distant. Views from the carriage window encompassing the rural scenery such as captured here, must have heightened the anticipation of those who had used the line to travel down from the Midlands for their annual visit to the beaches and sunshine of the South Coast. For that thought alone, this view is included!

Sturminster Marshall (Bailey Gate)

Serving Sturminster Marshall, the station was originally given that name but was renamed Bailey Gate in 1863, probably to avoid confusion with Sturminster Newton, opened in the same year. Station Road (running along the bottom right of the picture) crossed over the line on Bridge 220 – now replaced by the roundabout. The platforms sat alongside the current treeline in roughly the position of the closer industrial units. The goods yard has also provided space for further redevelopment and the industrial estate occupied the site of the former milk factory. Bailey Gate's proximity to the United

Dairies site resulted in considerable amounts of milk traffic sent to the London markets over S&D metals. This was originally routed via Wimborne but, with the closure of the direct route to that town in 1933, it was sent north to Templecombe. Inevitably, public houses noted on historical OS maps of the line are still in existence today. In this case the Churchill Arms – to the left of the former Bridge 220 – can be seen here (white building) for those thirsty for more knowledge and contemplating a site visit!

Bailey Gate Crossing & Corfe Mullen Junction

Sitting 1½ miles to the east of the station to which it gives its name, Bailey Gate Crossing took the line over the A31 Dorchester to Wimborne road. The signal box and crossing keeper's cottage have now gone (the latter only recently) but, in their place, sits a new residential building. Happily, the name 'Bailey Gate Crossing' has been retained.

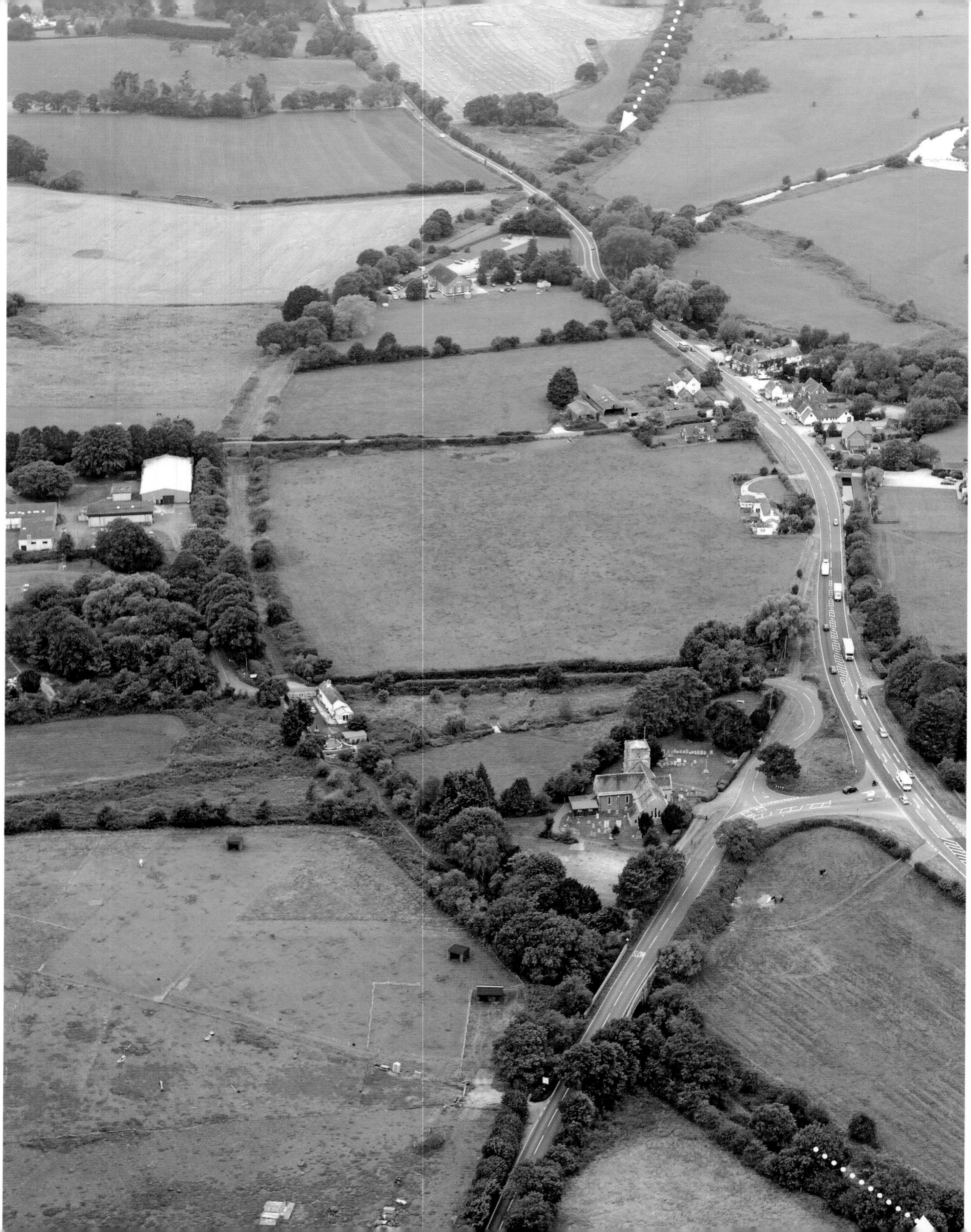

LEFT Such has been the expansion in housing around the Poole area that Corfe Mullen today encompasses a swathe of land towards the town's extremities. In S&D days Corfe Mullen was simply the tiny village seen here to the north of the line and bisected by the modern A31. After leaving Bailey Gate (Sturminster Marshall), southbound trains crossed the A31 at Bailey Gate Crossing, seen towards the top of the picture. In a sweeping curve to the east the line passed beneath Bridge 221 as it ran past the pumping station owned by Poole Corporation Water Works. A gated crossing by the white buildings allowed road access to Knoll Farm and also marked the site of Corfe Mullen Junction. The line passes out of view beneath Bridge 223 which carries the B3074 towards Broadstone and Poole.

ABOVE The A31 runs to the right of this shot carrying road traffic towards Wimborne. The original Dorset Central Railway also continued east for 3¾ miles to join the L&SWR at Wimborne via a trailing junction. This meant another inconvenient reversal for both north and southbound S&D trains. Therefore, in 1884/5, a new single line cut off was built from Corfe Mullen direct to Broadstone, where it again joined the L&SWR. This is the site of Corfe Mullen Junction. Today, the crossing keeper's cottage still exists – complete with a restored set of crossing gates. In 1933 the original route to Wimborne was truncated although a mile of track gave access to Carter's Siding clay pits. St Hubert's church is also prominent in this view.

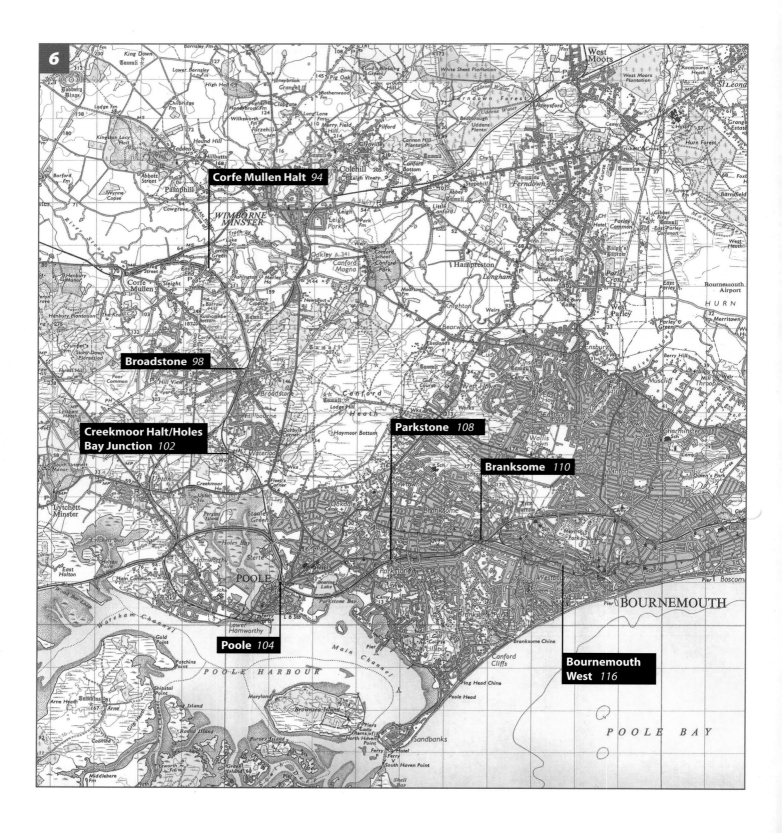

6

Corfe Mullen Halt *94*

Broadstone *98*

Creekmoor Halt/Holes Bay Junction *102*

Parkstone *108*

Branksome *110*

Poole *104*

Bournemouth West *116*

Bournemouth West was the destination for many of those travelling on the Somerset & Dorset, particularly holidaymakers from the Midlands. Here the original S&D part of the station, with its ornate awning, greets travellers, c1962. *Michael Blackbourn, courtesy of Mike Morant*

Corfe Mullen Halt

At Corfe Mullen Junction the S&D turned south out of the Stour Valley, climbing steeply at 1 in 80 to Corfe Mullen Halt. Inevitably, time has helped to trace the railway's path from the air as treelines have grown along the track formation. Careful study towards the top of the picture will reveal St Hubert's church and the line can be seen paralleling the A31 as Corfe Mullen Junction is passed. The old direct line to Wimborne continues and passes out of view to the right, leaving the new cut off to Broadstone sweeping towards the centre of the shot. Built as a result of local pressure, Corfe Mullen Halt opened in 1928 only to close in 1956. Situated in a deep cutting to the south of Bridge 235 (carrying the Wimborne road over the line), it had no shelter or facilities, with access gained via steps from the bridge. The cutting is now infilled but the site of the halt can be identified using the tall set of trees set across the trackbed by the roadway. The parapets of Bridge 236 (Lambs Green Lane) still stand, set just to the left of the adjacent cleared area (although hidden by trees in this view).

Now descending, the line bisects Broadstone Golf Course – its path still traced by trees – before entering the built up area on the outskirts of Poole at Broadstone Junction. The bottom right of this picture is worth noting – the triple-arch Bridge 238 still stands, although hidden from the airborne camera by trees. In the far distance Brownsea Island is embraced by the waters of Poole Harbour with the Purbecks forming a natural backdrop to the entire scene.

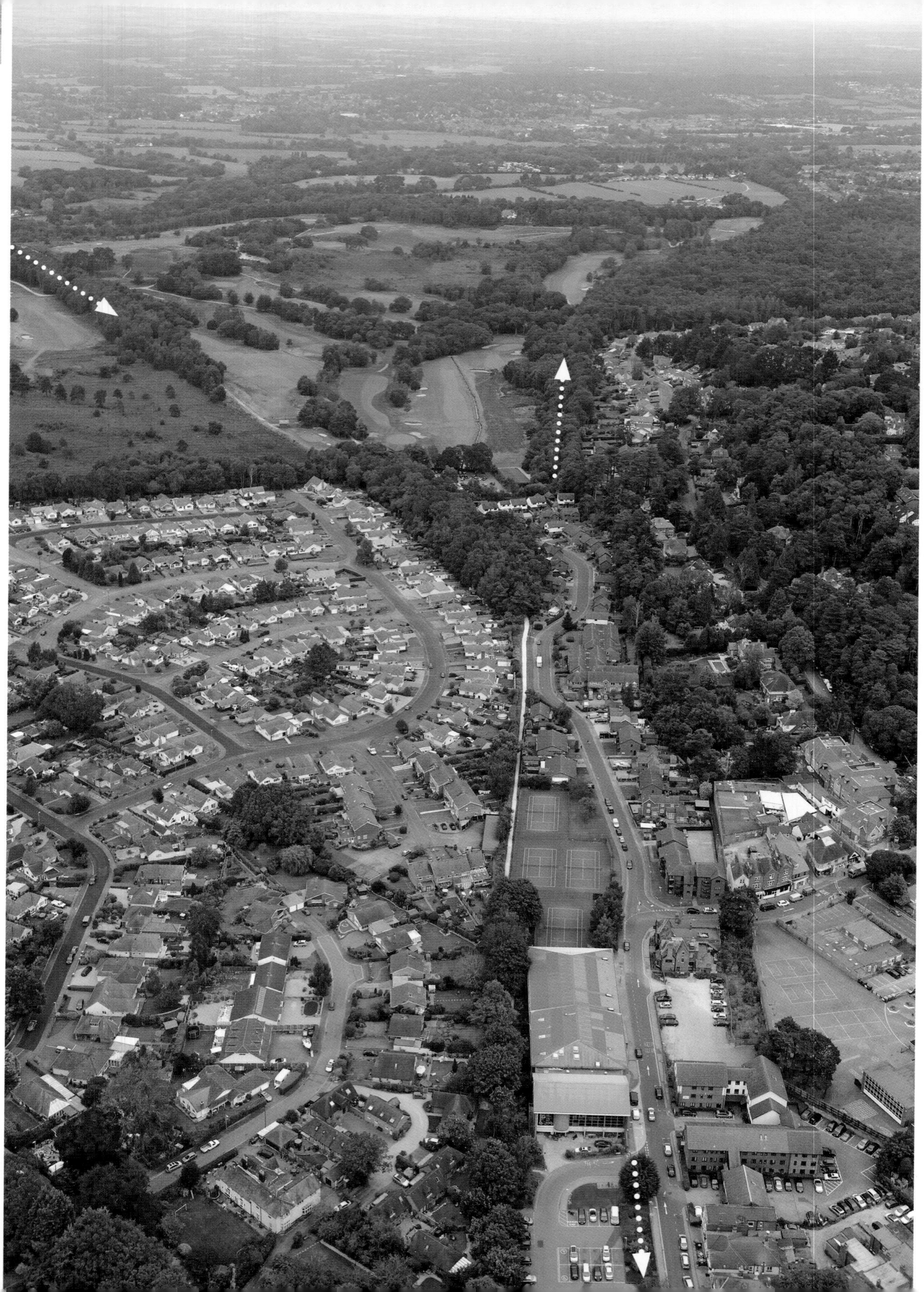

Broadstone

LEFT Broadstone Junction, 63 miles from Bath Road Junction, marked the end of S&D metals. From this point, trains travelled over L&SWR metals for the remaining 8 miles to Bournemouth. Originally running into Wimborne (seen here as the built up area at the top of the picture), S&D trains reversed and then ran via Broadstone to Hamworthy, near Poole. As described, the Corfe Mullen cut off allowed this reversal to be abandoned. With the opening of the L&SWR line from Broadstone (via Holes Bay Junction) to the new through station at Poole in 1872, the journey was further streamlined. Two years later the line reached Bournemouth West. Sitting high above Broadstone Station site (marked by the sports centre and car park), the S&D line can be seen swinging into the junction from the golf course to the left of shot. Less distinct – but still apparent from the air – the L&SWR line follows the treeline out towards Wimborne.

ABOVE Broadstone was a busy and important interchange station handling trains to Salisbury, Wimborne and Brockenhurst as well as S&D traffic. It also saw traffic from Weymouth, Dorchester and Waterloo until the Holes Bay curve opened in 1893. Built with four platforms and a substantial covered footbridge, all traces of this infrastructure have been swept away and today the site is occupied by a sports/leisure centre, car park and roundabout. (Some of the station's wooden structure was saved and has been re-erected at Medstead & Four Marks on the preserved Mid Hants Railway.) Fortunately, the former Railway Hotel – situated to the right of the sports centre in this view – survives as the Goods Yard public house and retains a degree of railway inspired atmosphere inside!

Broadstone station site occupies the centre of this view as the camera looks towards Poole and Hamworthy in the distance. The L&SWR line from Wimborne runs straight into the station site from the bottom of the shot while the S&D cut off from Corfe Mullen joins from the right, crossing L&SWR over metals and regaining double track as it does so. Looking beyond the sports centre, both sets of tracks then followed the path taken by today's roadway, lined by trees, as it continues south.

After leaving Broadstone S&D traffic for Bournemouth descended at 1 in 75 towards Holes Bay Junction. The Hamworthy line ran in parallel (but was singled in1932) before branching off towards the left side of this shot. The road today follows the path of the S&D's track formation. Broadstone Station site can just be seen at the top of this picture.

Creekmoor Halt/Holes Bay Junction

Continuing the southbound descent from Broadstone (looking north and out of sight, top right) the aptly named Broadstone Way takes advantage of the former trackbed as it sweeps down towards Poole, passing under the dual carriage way that is the A3049 Dorset Way. Just seen within the right hand side of this shot is the site of Creekmoor Halt. Opened in 1933, it was built using typically Southern pre-cast concrete components. A level crossing over a minor road at the northern end of the halt had hand worked gates. As can be seen here, urban expansion has been extensive. Had the railway remained, such an arrangement would prove unworkable today!

Over the years extensive land reclamation around the Poole area has altered the landscape. At the same time, urban development has meant that industrial units and retail stores cover the railway's former land. Looking south towards Poole the road continues to follow the trackbed as it passes under the modern bypass (crossing left to right). At this point the railway continued south through the site of today's B&Q store to join the L&SWR line seen crossing Holes Bay. Poole town centre is dominated by the triple towers of Barclays House with Poole station lying in their shadow. Of note is the broad expanse of Poole Harbour, Brownsea Island and the Purbecks beyond. Old Harry Rocks lie off the tip of the peninsula. Just over the Purbecks lies Swanage and – for those seeking steam and nostalgia – the Swanage Railway!

Poole

LEFT From the ground, Poole's skyline is dominated by the triple towers of Barclays House. This isn't so apparent from the air, although the building does provide a good reference point. Poole station is built on a sharp curve – a SWT Desiro '444' conveniently marks the site. The station's goods yard has been taken over by car parks although some siding space remains and is in use here by engineering stock. In S&D days trains leaving Poole were faced with two level crossings within a hundred yards. The first, Towngate, has now been replaced by the concrete overbridge carrying road traffic. The other, High Street, is now pedestrianised and is visible above the rooftop car park belonging to the Dolphin Shopping Centre. Poole retains a busy working quay (with ferry connections to the Channel Islands and Continent) as seen in the background.

ABOVE A closer view of Poole station confirms that the station infrastructure has been rebuilt several times over the years. The latest changes date from 1988 but it should be noted that in S&D days the buildings were situated on the platforms much closer to Towngate crossing. Interestingly, a condition of the S&D's running rights over L&SWR metals stated that all trains – even the 'Pines Express' – were required to stop at Poole station.

LEFT After leaving Poole station the line crosses Poole Park. Comparisons with earlier photographs will reveal the amount of land reclamation that has taken place. The London-bound '444' marks the passage of the line through the built up area. As suggested, Barclays House provides a convenient reference point.

ABOVE Having traced the S&D's path from Bath – often using just treelines and overgrown track formations – the opportunity to use a real train in order to follow the railway's final few miles towards Bournemouth is too good to miss! As Poole Bay is left behind, the climb of Parkstone bank begins in earnest. Much of the next two miles will be at 1 in 60 and even today's modern '444s' can find the going difficult if railhead conditions are bad.

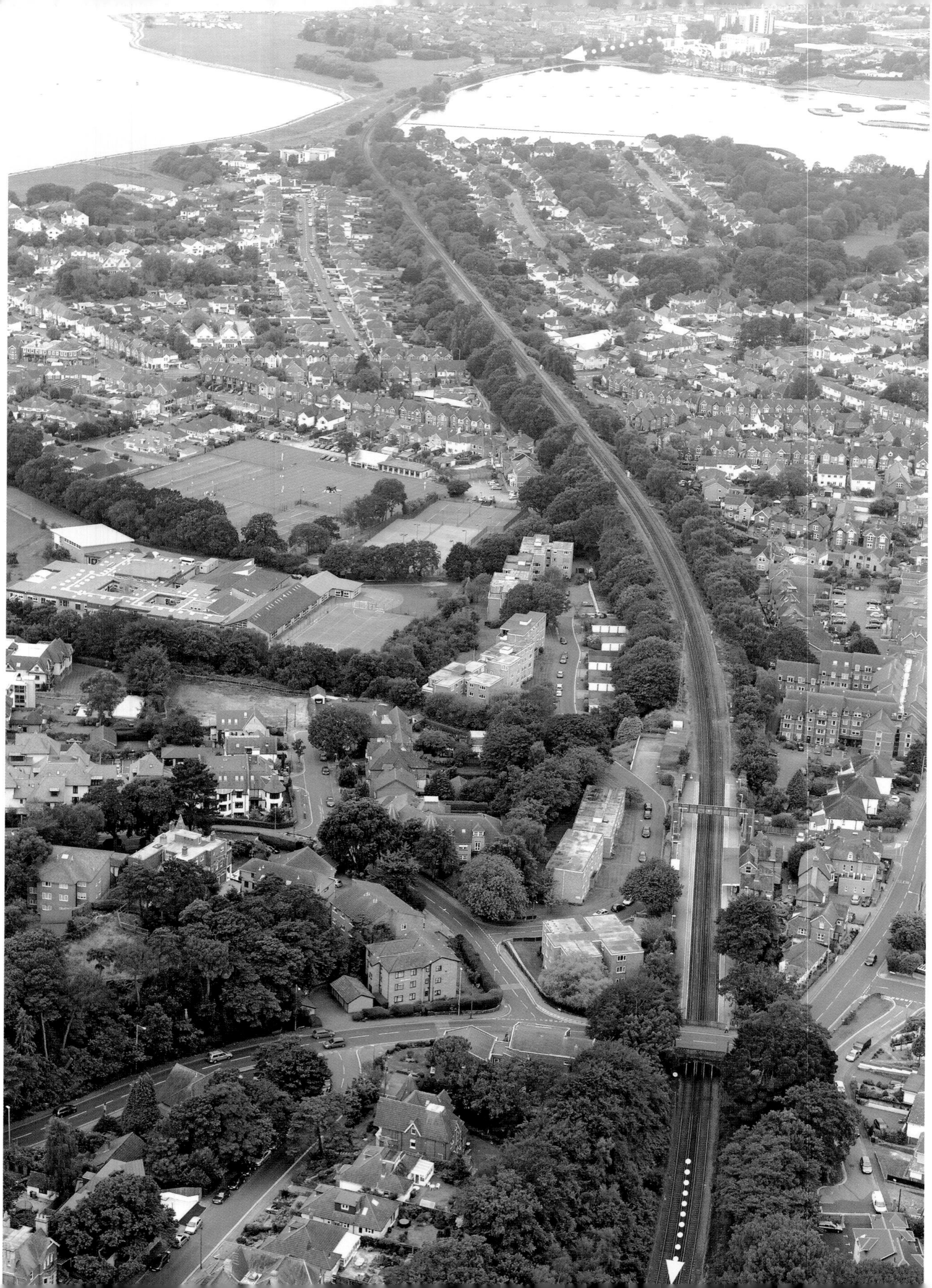

Parkstone

LEFT Poole sits at the top of this picture as the camera looks back down the first half of Parkstone bank. Anyone who has read Peter Smith's excellent *Footplate Over the Mendips* will recall tales of the final effort required – after almost 71 miles of challenging gradients – to crest the summit at Branksome before arriving into Bournemouth West. Having read of this as a schoolboy living in the northeast during the 1970s, little did I imagine experiencing the thrill of travelling on *Tangmere*'s footplate as she stormed through Parkstone station on a rail tour in 2012. The station sits just beyond the road overbridge. One can only imagine the sights and sounds that must have been commonplace here with a succession of steam-hauled trains – many banked – labouring up the incline. At the same time, others would race downhill en route to Weymouth or Bath and the Midlands via the S&D.

ABOVE Located midway between Poole and Branksome, Parkstone station is still open to traffic. The gradient eases briefly through station limits but immediately resumes at 1 in 60 until the summit is reached at Branksome. The former hotel attached to the station buildings has now been renovated and reopened as 'The Cow'. Painted grey, it has a useful open balcony should anyone find themselves in the area as a steam special is passing en route to or from the delights of Swanage or Weymouth!

Branksome

LEFT Looking to the east, the physical boundary between Poole and Bournemouth is indistinct. Bournemouth town centre and seafront runs across the top of the picture. The climb out of Poole for southbound trains continues until Branksome station is reached. From here S&D traffic took the right-hand fork at the junction whilst London traffic continued left towards Bournemouth Central – as demonstrated by the '444' just leaving Branksome. Also clearly visible from the air are the carriage and maintenance sheds of Bournemouth Traincare Depot.

ABOVE A closer view of Branksome station shows that access remains via steps from the covered footbridge. Trains cresting Parkstone bank arrived from left of shot with the junction for Bournemouth West appearing on the right side of the picture by the track worker seen in hi-vis orange. Incidentally, it is interesting to note how readily he stands out – essential on today's high speed railway. Compare this with track gangs working on or near the running line in S&D days!

ABOVE Using the hi-vis track workers as a link from the previous photograph, the eastern junction of the Bournemouth triangle is seen here. Trains to London would take the upper line towards Bournemouth Central whilst S&D traffic branched right towards journey's end at Bournemouth West. On the extreme left of the picture the site of the former Branksome signal box controlling the junction can be seen. Only the brick retaining wall now remains.

RIGHT Central to this scene are the modern carriage sheds and washing plant at Bournemouth Traincare Depot. On passing the carriage stabling sidings in S&D days, trains arriving from Bath had a final ¼ mile of 1 in 90 to descend before arriving at Bournemouth West. Looking towards the top of the picture it is possible to follow the path of the line around the curve at Branksome and down Parkstone bank towards Poole.

The northernmost junction of the Bournemouth triangle was known as Gas Works Junction. This allowed trains from Bournemouth Central to run to Bournemouth West. Taken out of use in 1965, Bournemouth West Curve is now overgrown with weeds and the track has been lifted. It was notorious for the difficulty involved in starting heavy trains from rest on the sharp curve if checked by signals. The two large viaducts allowing the railway to cross the deep Bourne Valley remain although only one is in use as can clearly be seen from the air. The middle of the triangle contained a goods yard and the S&D two-road locomotive shed, coaling stage and turntable. Branksome Shed, an outpost of Midland practice deep within Southern territory, stood in the area now occupied by the parked cars at the top of this picture.

From height the geography of the S&D's southern limits can be seen. Bournemouth Triangle sits in the centre of this shot. It also allowed locomotives to be turned if they were too large for Branksome Shed's turntable. Indeed, traffic from Bournemouth Shed also turned here with advantage taken by coupling several locomotives together to turn en masse around the triangle rather than individually on shed when traffic was heavy. Looking beyond the modern traincare depot the A338

Wessex Way can be seen encroaching upon the former trackbed as Bournemouth West is approached. Meanwhile, the L&SWR London line sweeps around the town's northern extremities towards Bournemouth Central station (now known simply as Bournemouth). Although not visible from this aerial perspective, it is interesting to note the relative distance of each station from the town's centre. And then to consider which one has survived and is in use today!

Bournemouth West

ABOVE A closer view of the area reveals that nothing now remains as a link with the former station. Interestingly, Bournemouth West didn't just handle S&D traffic. It was also the starting point and destination for trains to Weymouth, Swanage, West Moors, Brighton and London Waterloo.

RIGHT Bournemouth West was officially closed in 1965. It had no less than six platforms which were provided with canopies although there was no overall station roof. The station entrance was south facing, occupying the area now taken up with the four parked cars. In this shot the A338 Wessex Way now cuts through the station site. Only the former Midland Hotel remains recognisable, albeit with difficulty as it is masked by scaffolding in this view.

COLE
One of the Armstrong Whitworth constructed 4F 0-6-0s, No 44559, has just crossed the ex Great Western line and is letting the gradient slow the Bath to Templecombe train for its stop at Cole on 11 August 1962 not even disturbing the cattle in the foreground. *Mark Warburton*

COLE
The afternoon winter sunshine on 1 February 1964 illuminates BR Standard Class 5MT No 73051 and its train leaving Cole station. The engine came new to Bath Green Park from Derby in 1954 and stayed there until withdrawn in August 1965, acquiring the BR Green livery after overhaul at Eastleigh in September 1963.
Mark Warburton

WINCANTON

Rebuilt 'West Country' No 34046 Braunton has charge of the Up 'Pines Express' on 6 August 1962, seen here at Wincanton. The staggered platforms enable a clear view along the 12 coaches showing the changes in gradient that resulted from the avoiding of expensive earthworks in the construction of the extension of the original Highbridge to Glastonbury line of the Somerset Central Railway to Templecombe.

Mark Warburton

WINCANTON

BR Standard Class 5MT No 73001 is glimpsed through the door of the Wincanton goods shed as it restarts the 9.50am Bath to Bournemouth service on 6 December 1965. The sidings in the foregound show that little private trafffic has been handled since the closure of the goods service in April 1965.

Mark Warburton

TEMPLECOMBE
Ivatt 2-6-2T No 41291 pilots BR 2-6-0 No 76014 into Templecombe Upper station with a Bournemouth to Bath train on 6 November 1965. No 41291 was attached at Templecombe Junction to reverse the train into the Upper station. On departing 76014 will use the crossover visible under 41291 to cross to the Up Main line passing Templecombe Junction towards Bath. *Mark Warburton*

TEMPLECOMBE
BR Standard Class 4 2-6-4T No 80138 has arrived at Templecombe Upper with the 8.15am Bath to Templecombe on Thursday 3 March 1966 in the last week of operation of the Somerset & Dorset and passenger services at Templecombe station. The photographer had chased this train by car, Ivo Peters' style, photographing it previously at Shepton Mallet, Evercreech Junction and Horsington. No 41206 is on pilot duty in front of the signalbox, which is happily still with us as part of the station which was reopened in 1983 after pressure and much work by the local community. *Mark Warburton*

TEMPLECOMBE
On the penultimate day of public service, Friday 4 March 1966, Ivatt 2-6-2T No 41290 pilots a Bournemouth to Templecombe service hauled by BR Standard Class 4 2-6-4T No 80085 from Templecombe Junction to Templecombe Upper station. Templecombe Junction signalbox can be seen on the right-hand edge of the picture beyond the locomotive shed and with 43 levers was the largest on the Somerset & Dorset. *Mark Warburton*

TEMPLECOMBE
Templecombe shed from Coombe Throop Lane bridge over the Bournemouth line on 11 September 1960 when the Stephenson Locomotive Society special ran from Bath to Templecombe with a visit to the shed. '2P' 4-4-0 No 40537 in the foreground, which was to survive a further 18 months, was a former Midland locomotive with right-hand drive and 7ft driving wheels whereas Nos 40565 further up the siding and 40564 on the right are left-hand drive 6ft 9in driving wheel engines from 1928. Also in evidence are Ivatt 2-6-2 tanks and Fowler 4F 0-6-0s. *Mark Warburton1*

HENSTRIDGE

Henstridge was the smallest station on the line and by the date of this photograph, 4 March 1966, the goods siding had been lifted. It was not a block station and the lever frame was located in the station building – the gap in the platform for the point rodding can still be seen. *Mark Warburton*

HENSTRIDGE

BR 2-6-4T No 80085 leaves Henstridge on 3 March 1966 with the 9.37am from Bournemouth Central to Templecombe, passing the site of the goods siding.

Mark Warburton

STALBRIDGE

BR 4-6-0 No 75073 restarts the 12.30pm Templecombe to Bournemouth service from Stalbridge station on 16 December 1965. This was the first crossing place on the single line south from Templecombe and the standard of the Whitaker Tablet-Exchanging Apparatus can be seen in the left foreground.
Mark Warburton

STURMINSTER NEWTON

BR 2-6-0 No 76061 rolls into Sturminster Newton on 19 April 1965 with an afternoon up train from Bournemouth. Judging by the coats of the passengers awaiting the down train, it is a chilly day. *Mark Warburton*

SHILLINGSTONE

Shillingstone station is seen from the Templecombe end on 2 March 1966. Unusually for Dorset Central Railway wayside stations it had an awning but shared with Midsomer Norton a distinctly horticultural bent among its staff and their greenhouse is visible just to the left of the awning supports. Happily the building has survived and is now being restored by the North Dorset Railway Trust.
Mark Warburton

SHILLINGSTONE

BR 4-6-0 No 73054 on the Easter Monday Bristol to Bournemouth excursion, 23 April 1962, waits at Shillingstone station to cross an up train. Mark Warburton knows he has time to photograph the train and get back on board before the engine crew have the single line tablet for the Shillingstone to Blandford Forum section. *Mark Warburton*

BLANDFORD

BR 4-6-0 No 75072 takes water at Blandford Forum on an up (Templecombe bound) train on 11 December 1965. *Mark Warburton*

BLANDFORD

A south easterly view of the goods yard at Blandford Forum on 3 March 1966 still shows evidence of considerable traffic. There is much here which gives the character of the steam age station chimney smoking from the stove in the Porters' Room; barrows on the platforms; domestic coal being put into sacks in the foreground. *Mark Warburton*

BAILEY GATE
BR 2-6-4T No 80085 enters Bailey Gate station on 3 March 1966 with the 12.30pm from Templecombe to Bournemouth. A siding to the Unigate Creameries was added here in 1955 on the Bournemouth side of the station and rail traffic continued to it until May 1968.
Mark Warburton

CORFE MULLEN
A rather weary and run down BR 2-6-0, No 76026, passes Corfe Mullen Junction signalbox northbound on 4 March 1966. The ancient parish church of St Hubert's on the left dates from the 13th century so has seen the railway come and go. *Mark Warburton*

BROADSTONE
While BR 2-6-0 No 76005 awaits the right away on 2 March 1966, the layout at Broadstone is revealed. The train is standing on the double track from Holes Bay Junction near Poole and the train is signalled across the double junctions onto the single track line to Corfe Mullen Junction. The double track on the left of the picture leads to Hamworthy Junction in the Weymouth direction and to Wimborne and Ringwood in the up direction.
Mark Warburton

BOURNEMOUTH WEST
BR 2-6-0 No 76026 stands in Bournemouth West station on 3 February 1965 with a train to Templecombe carrying the SDJR lamp headcode for a passenger train. Bournemouth West closed completely on 4 October 1965 and all passenger trains were diverted to Bournemouth Central.
Mark Warburton

The reason why! Mile upon mile of sandy beaches made Bournemouth a popular destination for holidaymakers travelling from the Midlands and further north via the S&D. Both Bournemouth and Poole are visible together from the air, as are some of the railway landmarks identified in previous pages. The views experienced on the journey south from Bath, when seen from above, have been spectacular and the journey time much shorter than the railway traveller might have experienced. Despite this saving most people would relish the chance to travel the route behind steam if it were possible. Looking at these remarkable photographs, it is only too clear why the Somerset & Dorset Railway is still held in such great affection today!